SONG *of a*
LONGING HEART

SONG of a
LONGING HEART

*Fresh Insights on Song of Solomon
from the Author of Psalm 23:
The Song of a Passionate Heart*

DAVID ROPER

Discovery House Publishers

Books, music, and videos that feed the soul with the Word of God

Box 3566 Grand Rapids, MI 49501

Discovery House Publishers is affiliated with RBC Ministries,
Grand Rapids, Michigan.

Discovery House books are distributed to the trade exclusively by
Barbour Publishing, Inc., Uhrichsville, Ohio.

Requests for permission to quote from this book should be directed to:
Permissions Department, Discovery House Publishers, P.O. Box 3566,
Grand Rapids, MI 49501.

Unless otherwise indicated, Scripture quotations are from the *New
International Version*® NIV® © 1973, 1978, 1984 by International Bible
Society. Used by permission of The Zondervan Corporation. The "NIV"
and "New International Version" trademarks are registered in the United
States Patent and Tradmark Office by International Bible Society.

Library of Congress Cataloging-in-Publication Data

Roper, David
Song of a longing heart : fresh insights on the song of Solomon /
    David Roper.
        cm.
ISBN 1-57293-139-6
1. Bible. O.T. Song of Solomon—Criticism, interpretation, etc. 2.
    Marriage—Biblical teaching. 3. Love—Biblical teaching. 4.
    Sex—Biblical teaching. 5. Marriage—Religious aspects—Chris-
    tianity. 6. Love—Religious aspects—Christianity. 7. Sex—Reli-
    gious aspects—Christianity. I. Title.
BS1485.6.M3R67 2005
223' . 906—dc22   2005005364

Printed in the United States of America
05 06 07 08 09 / BPI / 10 9 8 7 6 5 4 3 2 1

Carolyn…

You have stolen my heart, my sister, my bride;
You have stolen my heart with one glance of your eyes.
Song of Songs 4:9

CONTENTS

THE SONG

SONG *of a* LONGING HEART

THE WAY I SEE IT

He bends down   their lips   to kiss,

Behold,   their lips   are sweet,

sweet   as grapes

UGARITIC TEXT 52:49,50

I recall a character from the underground comics of the 1960s, Robert Crumb's "Mr. Natural" of "keep on truckin'" fame. Mr. Natural's social comments provided a shrewd, although often profane, analysis of that era. One of his comic segments sticks in my mind: A boy watches a mini-skirted young woman walk by and asks, "Mr. Natural, is sex the answer?"

"No my boy," Mr. Natural replies, "sex is the question."

Indeed. Sex has always been the question. Despite the current sex-information glut and emphasis on "anything goes" erotica, sex is still a mystery, our single greatest hang-up. "People now seem to have sex on their minds," Malcolm Muggeridge said, "which is a peculiar place to have it." Our fixation with sex is indeed a misplacing of it.

But, you say, "We know more about human sexuality than ever before. We have manuals, methods, and techniques that make for great sex"— which is exactly the problem. When men and women no longer know "why," they settle on "how"—on technique, which is why we have such a spate of sex manuals these days (*101 Days of Great Sex, The New Joy of Sex, Best Sex You've Ever Had,* and thousands more). But for all of our methods, we have lost the meaning of sex itself. And in an odd and anguished way, deep inside us, we know it.

G. K. Chesterton compares us to a shipwrecked sailor, marooned on a desert island and suffering from amnesia. As remnants of the ship and relics from his former life drift ashore, the sailor combs the beach, retrieving each bit and piece of his past, trying to remember its intended purpose. He experiments with each item but misuses it because he's forgotten what it is for. Chesterton would say that sex is one of those relics left over from an earlier state of being, the purpose of which we've largely forgotten.

We speak of sex as beautiful because we know it ought to be, but what should be beautiful has become ugly and dull. For many, the sex act is just that—an act, little more than aimless coupling, having little or nothing to do with the deeper currents of life and love that truly satisfy.[1] There's little romance or intimacy, only hunger, heartache, and misery. That which ought to take away our loneliness only adds to it. Like the old Rolling Stones, we "can't get no satisfaction" though we've "tried and tried and tried."[2]

Where is this "great sex," everywhere advertised and promoted but nowhere found? Where is this elusive grail for which we search?

It cannot be discovered; it must be disclosed. And one such disclosure is an old love song buried deep in the heart of the Old Testament—a strange and beautiful collection of poems known as the Song of Solomon, or more accurately, Solomon's Song of Songs (that is to say, "The Incomparable Song," the greatest of songs).

Years ago, when I was a student in the Ancient Near Eastern Studies Department at the University of California at Berkeley, I spent most of one year studying Ugaritic literature. (Ugaritic is an ancient Northwest Semitic language, the language of ancient Canaan, and a close linguistic relative of biblical Hebrew.) In due time we began to study Ugaritic poetry—erotic love

---

[1] A student who submitted himself to Alfred Kinsey's inquiries said afterward that, no matter what answers he gave to the questions, Kinsey kept asking him, "Yes, but how many times?" Sex was reduced to an act and the act to a merely quantitative measurement of it.

[2] It is significant that we say we lust *after* something or someone. Lust is always in pursuit and never satisfied. In Dante's *Inferno*, the lustful run around the Blessed Mountain in opposite directions. They embrace each other quickly as they pass, "not pausing with this brief salute content." One brief erotic encounter and they move on to another.

poetry actually[3]—and I discovered to my surprise that many of the similes, analogies, and other literary forms and figures of speech in Solomon's Song of Songs are also found in this material.

I came to the conclusion that the Song, on a literal level, is a collection of delightful love poems celebrating pure marital love, and as such, was God's response to the degraded sexual practices of the Canaanites[4] and an apologetic for biblical sexual morality. Moreover, since "all Scripture is God-breathed and is *useful* for teaching, rebuking, correcting and training in righteousness,"[5] I came to see that the traditional allegorical and mystical method of interpreting the Song of Songs is not only credible, but "useful,"—useful in that it enabled God's covenant people to understand their sexuality and put it to its intended purpose. The Song serves the same purpose for God's people today. Taken at face value this book is a richly detailed love song, a bold celebration of physical beauty, intimacy, and passion. But it is more. It is an answer to our search for the meaning of sex and human sexuality.

Poets are notoriously difficult to interpret. They may, in fact, intend their symbols to be understood in more than one way. This is no less true of biblical poetry. Thus my interpretation of the Song is simply mine—the way *I* see it.

DHR

---

[3] See the Appendix for an example of this Ugaritic poetry.

[4] It is worth noting that Canaanite morality was notoriously degraded. Their gods and goddesses were portrayed in the nude, in contrast to other Near Eastern religions that clothed their deities. Their religious poetry and ritual centered on violent and debasing sex acts, portraying every form of deviant sexuality conceived by the human race.

[5] 2 Timothy 3:16, emphasis added.

WHAT IS THIS SONG?

When he is young he has to look for his mate, and then he has to court her;
then he begets young; then he remembers all this and boils it inside him and
makes it into poems and wisdom.

— C. S. LEWIS, *Out of the Silent Planet*

The Song of Songs is arguably the most beautiful and poetic book in the Bible. It is also one of the most startling. Understood literally, it is a collection of erotic[1] love poems, a bold celebration of sexual passion—which raises the question: "What is this book doing in the Bible?"[2]

Early writers understood the Song to be an extended metaphor depicting our love for God and His love for us. For this reason, the book has been the favorite of some of Christianity's greatest saints and mystics, such as Saint Bernard of Clairvaux (1090–1153), who wrote eighty-six sermons on the Song,[3] and Thomas Aquinas (1225–1274), who was writing a commentary on it when he died. The Spanish Carmelite mystic, St. John of the Cross (1542–1591), wrote a poem on the deeper spiritual life entitled, "Cantico Espiritual," replete with symbols and phrases drawn directly from the Latin translation of the Song. And in more recent times, many have been greatly enriched by Jesse Penn-Lewis's booklet, *The Hidden Ones,* based on the Song of Songs.

This interpretation answers, in part, the question of why the Song of Songs is the only book in the Bible (except for the book of Esther) that never once mentions God. The answer is that God is found everywhere in

---

[1] "Erotic" is from a Greek word *eros* which refers primarily to "falling in love," or infatuation as well as sexual passion. *Eros* has now become associated almost exclusively with sexual desire, but this was not its original meaning. (See the chapter on "The Logic of Infatuation.")

[2] I once saw a cartoon in a magazine depicting three young Israelis reading a scroll of the *Song of Songs.* An elderly Jewish matron standing nearby scowls and says to a friend, "I don't care if Solomon is the king. I still think it's a dirty book!"

[3] These sermons covered little more than the first two chapters of the Song.

symbol and song. The bridegroom is a symbol for God, and his chosen bride is a symbol for the human soul. Interpreted symbolically, this book describes in intimate detail the thing for which we hope and hunger: our meeting and marriage with God. When the bride cries out to the bridegroom, "Kiss me!" she is uttering the enduring hunger of every soul to be embraced and loved by infinite Love.

JEWISH INTERPRETATIONS

The earliest clear reference to the Song occurs in The Mishnah, a collection of rabbinic teaching on most points of the law, written down around AD 100 after a long oral tradition. In this work the Song is seen as a dialogue between the Lord of the World and the Congregation of Israel. The commentator asks, "How are the words, 'Thy love is better than wine' understood?" Then answers that the Groom's love is expressed through his Word "which is better than any other words."

The most complete Jewish commentary of the Song is an Aramaic paraphrase dated about AD 550, which again takes the poem as an allegory[4] of God's love for His people, beginning with the Exodus from Egypt and enduring despite their troubled existence throughout Israel's history.

The Jewish exegete, Rashi,[5] comments that "all the references to *Shlomo* [Solomon] [in the text] refer not only to King Shlomo, the son of David, but also to *HaShem* (*"The Name"*), as the King of the Universe Who Creates Peace in the Heavens. The name *Shlomo* is related to the word *Shalom* meaning Peace, that is in fact one of the Names of *HaShem*, because this Song is the holiest of all the Songs that have been sung by human beings to *HaShem*." Rashi believed that the book was written to show Israel that God "has not afflicted her willingly; that though he did send her away, he has not cast her off; that she is still his wife and he her husband, and that he will be united to her."

---

[4] "In literature, an allegory is an extended metaphor in which characters, objects, incidents, and descriptions carry one or more sets of fully developed meanings in addition to the apparent and literal ones." Thus it represents one thing in the guise of another. John Bunyan's *Pilgrim's Progress* is an example of this. (*Benet's Reader's Encyclopedia,* 3rd edition [New York: Harper & Row Publishers, 1987], 25.)

[5] RASHI is an acronym for Rabbi Shlomo ben Yitzchak, an eleventh century rabbi, who was considered by Jews to be the greatest commentator on the Written Law and Oral Law.

There are other examples of this form of interpretation, all indicating that Jewish writers viewed the poem allegorically. However, allegory does not rule out a literal understanding of the text. In fact, it was characteristic of Jewish exegesis to base allegory on a solid foundation of literal interpretation. The rabbis never discarded the plain meaning of the text. To do so was contrary to the respect they accorded the Scriptures.

One student of rabbinics, R. P. C. Hanson, observed that the allegory of the rabbis "is characterized by the fact that it never for one moment impugns the validity of the literal sense."[6] Thus, the fact that rabbis allegorized the text does not rule out a more literal understanding of it. There are, in fact, a number of indications that the Song was also viewed in ancient times as a straightforward love poem.

One such indication is the nature of the debate over its continued inclusion in the Jewish scriptures. We know from ancient Jewish sources that there was considerable discussion concerning whether the Song of Songs should remain in the Bible. If the poem had been understood solely as an allegory of God's love for Israel, its place in the Jewish scriptures would have been assured. But apparently the rabbis at that early date concluded that the poem at its most fundamental level was a love poem and thus the question arose, "Should this work *remain* in the Bible?" (It is significant that the debate over the Song has never been over whether it should be included in the canon of Scripture, but whether it should *remain*.)

The Council at Jamnia (c. AD 100) settled the issue of the Song's inclusion in the Jewish canon, though clearly it was considered a part of Scripture long before the council met. It's generally agreed that Jamnia did not establish the Song's place but merely verified it. However, the question of interpretation continued to create problems on a more practical level. Rabbi Aqiba defended the Song with these words, "For in the entire world, there is nothing to equal the day on which the Song of Solomon was given to Israel. All the writings are holy but the Song of Songs is the most holy." And he also rebuked those who sang "the *Song of Songs* in wine taverns, treating it as if it were a vulgar song."[7] That this practice existed at all suggests that the

---

[6] Richard Patrick Hansen, *Allegory and Event* (Richmond: John Knox Press, 1959).

[7] "Tosaphta," *Sanhedrin, The Mishna Treatise Sanhedrin* (Leiden: E. J. Brill, 1909).

Song, though interpreted on one level as an allegory, on another level was taken quite literally.

CHRISTIAN INTERPRETATIONS

Having noted the effective way in which Jewish scholars and teachers interpreted the Song as an allegory, many early Christians interpreted the Song of Songs in the same manner. Augustine (354–430), the early church father, and Jerome (374–419), who translated the Bible into the common Latin of the day, both championed allegorical understandings of the poems.

Such interpretation found its fullest and most influential expression in Bernard of Clairvaux's eighty-six sermons on the Song of Songs, where he equates the Beloved with the individual soul seeking God. Bernard saw this collection of poems as the very heart of the spiritual life, an interpretation that continued unabated for centuries. The frequency with which spiritual commentaries on the Song appear in monastic libraries during this period attests to its popularity and use in cultivating the spiritual life.[8]

The translators of the King James Bible (1611), perhaps the most beautiful version of the poem in the English language, virtually canonized the allegorical approach with their interpretive headings. For example, the heading for the first chapter reads, "The Church's love unto Christ," while the second chapter is entitled, "The mutual love of Christ and his Church." And "The Church having a taste of Christ's love" is the interpretive explanation for the verse "My beloved put in his hand by the hole of the door, and my bowels were moved for him."

Since that time most translations of the Bible have followed their lead. The Jerusalem Bible, published in 1966, ends its introduction to the Song with these words: "Whatever theory of interpretation we adopt we are justified in applying the Song to the mutual love of Christ and his Church or to the union of the individual soul with God. Mystics like St John of the Cross were wise to use the Song as they did."

---

[8] St. Hippolytus of Rome (AD 200) provides the earliest surviving Christian commentary on the poems, a commentary that deeply influenced the allegorist, Origen (c. AD 250). Origen considered the Song one of the most important books in the Bible because it revealed how one's sexual drives could be sublimated. "Ever let the bridegroom (Christ) fondle you," he wrote. Eroticism was diverted into mysticism.

There is a strong rationale for these allegorical interpretations of the Song. Throughout Scripture, the biblical writers frequently use human romantic love and marriage as their chosen symbol for the love of God because marital love comprises the highest and best of human companionship, friendship, affection, desire, and self-sacrificing love. Even the apostle Paul insists that the physical union of husband and wife speaks of our spiritual union with Christ (Ephesians 5:31–32). I see no reason, however, why we must choose between symbolic and literal interpretations of this book.[9] It is possible to interpret a book or a passage symbolically and not abandon the literal sense of the text. Thus, the Song can be understood on two levels: horizontal and vertical, divine and human. The bridegroom symbolizes God, but he is also every man; the bride symbolizes the soul, but she is also every woman. As Paul would say, "This is a great mystery."[10]

Having said that, I hasten to add that taken literally the poem is *first* about human love and as such has a message to deliver quite apart from its allegorical meaning. (I must also stress that the Song of Songs focuses on a *married* couple and not on unmarried lovers.) Though we find analogies to all things spiritual in the images of the Song, I do not think the poems were written for that purpose alone. The meaning of the collection must first be sought in the plain and literal sense of the text and then in its mystical, metaphorical sense, an exegetical method to which we shall return later. I believe both methods of interpretation are essential to understand the depths of the Song.

THE INSCRIPTION

The best way to view Song of Songs, I believe, is to see it as a collection of individual love poems dealing with an idealized love story.[11] The complete

---

[9] Ephesians 5:32. St. Gregory observed, "Holy Writ by the manner of its speech transcends every science, because in one and the same sentence, while it describes a fact it reveals a mystery."

[10] "The interpretation is twofold. Primarily, the book is the expression of pure marital love as ordained of God in creation, and the vindication of that love as against both asceticism and lust—the two profanations of the holiness of marriage. The secondary and larger interpretation is of Christ, the Son and His heavenly side, the Church" (C. I. Scofield in his introduction to the Song of Solomon).

[11] I am not the first to view the Song this way. The German poet Herder suggested in 1846 that the Song is a collection of separate poems celebrating love.

title of the collection is "The Song of Songs which is Solomon's" (1:1), which comes from the opening words of the first verse *shir hasherim* (meaning "song of songs"). Ancient biblical "books" were actually scrolls, not books as we know them, and had no covers or title pages, so the first line identified what they were.

"Song of songs" is the Hebrew way of expressing the superlative degree of comparison, as in "slave of slaves" (Genesis 9:25), "God of gods" (Deuteronomy 10:17), "vanity of vanities" (Ecclesiastes 1:2), "holy of holies" (Exodus 26:33), and "king of kings" (Daniel 2:37). According to the inscription "song of songs," then, this is the greatest collection of songs ever assembled.

You might think it audacious of Solomon to describe his work in such grand terms. It's almost certain, however, that the title we find in our modern translations is not the original inscription, but was added later by an editor. The word translated "which" in the title verse is different from the synonym used for that pronoun every other place in the book, suggesting that the title and accolade were added later.

The phrase "which is Solomon's" suggests authorship, although in some contexts it may indicate nothing more than ownership, in which case, this could be a collection of poems written under Solomon's sponsorship, or a collection that was part of his personal collection of wisdom literature. The Hebrew preposition found here is used in the headings of many of the psalms ascribed to David ("A Psalm of David").

A good deal of ink has been spilled over the question of authorship of the Song, but I find the issue unimportant (although I do believe it can be attributed to King Solomon). The important thing is that the work can be attributed to a single author who had a specific purpose in mind, in contrast to an "editor" who simply pieced together unrelated poems.

However, there's no reason to deny Solomon credit for this work. The description of local events and circumstances, the imagery drawn from the royal court, the references to horses, the Tower of David, the Pools of Heshbon, the cities of Tirzah, the region of Gilead fit well with what we know of 10th century BC Israel. Recent scholarship also supports the view that the language comes from Solomon's time. Furthermore, Solomon's wisdom was legendary and his literary genius established by his other works, for, "he spoke three thousand proverbs and his songs numbered a thousand and five" (1 Kings 4:32).

And so, though only the title affirms it, I will assume that Solomon's wisdom is enshrined in the Song of Songs as it is in the other wisdom books of the Bible. It has been suggested that while Job explores the mystery of suffering and Ecclesiastes the mystery of existence, the Song of Songs explores the mystery of love. Solomon was, as the Bible assures us, the wisest man of his time. As such we have much to learn from him.

THE FORMAT

The poems in the Song do not represent a consecutive, connected narrative. In fact, as poets insist, love lyrics seldom tell a story; they only allude to one. In this collection, Solomon introduces two protagonists: himself, the "Lover" and his feminine counterpart, the "Beloved," elsewhere called the "Shulamite" (6:13).

"Shulamite" (*Shulamith* in Hebrew) is very close to the feminized form of Solomon's name (*Shlomoh*). If Solomon is intentionally using a contrived or coined feminine form of his own name, he may be making the same word play used by the author of Genesis when he observed that Adam's bride was called "woman" (*ishshah*) because she was taken from "man" (*ish*). The play on words in Genesis is not precise because *ishshah* (from the root *enosh*) is not the exact feminine form of the masculine *ish*, but the parallel is sufficient to convey the idea that woman was created to be man's counterpart.[12]

I do not know if Solomon intended to make a word play on his name as the author of Genesis played on the names of the original couple, but it's highly possible that he had that model in mind. If so, his purpose is to describe an ideal marital union—a husband and wife deeply (madly) in love.

THE STYLE

The environment of most of the poems in the Song is pastoral and rustic, though there is a mix of rural settings and urban court life. For example,

---

[12] The same near-pun exists in English. "Woman" is not a feminized form of the noun "man" but rather comes from Middle English "woof-man" or "man who weaves."

the lover is described in 1:7 as a shepherd while later he's depicted as an oriental king (3:6 ff.). This is confusing to us in the West, but a mingling of rural and urban contexts is common in Semitic literature.

Other stylistic techniques strike you at once. There is a changing pattern, a shifting of mood, subject matter, and locale. The organization of the poems suggests a "stream-of-consciousness," designed to evoke certain impressions and moods rather than transmit precise data.

Another feature of the poetic style of the Song is what literary critic C. S. Lewis called "golden poetry," which through richness of imagery and metaphor arouses a sensory and emotional response. Romance is depicted as an experience with sensuous thrills of sight, hearing, aroma, touch and taste. The poems are filled with images of field and flower, with ideally ardent lovers walking hand in hand through idealized landscapes. The secret of these symbols lies in their subtlety, in a delicate eroticism portrayed in symbols that evoke emotional reactions. The aim of the poet is not to produce an exact and detailed description of events. We're invited to *feel* what the lovers felt rather than observe what they did.

The most obvious feature of the poems is that the lovers speak of their physical love in symbolism and metaphor. The language is restrained, delicate, and sensitive, even when it is most sensuous. This use of indirect symbols, which conceal even as they reveal, heightens the charm of the sentiments expressed. The description of love and lovemaking is neither crass nor clinical. As a result, we receive strong impressions without being asked to picture everything in graphic detail.

In the words of seventeenth-century English poet Robert Herrick, the Song contains a "cleanly wantonness." The lovers seem new to love, tender and full of the wonder of discovery, with passion and yet purity in their delight in each other.

THE LANGUAGE AND THE TEXT

In the next section of this book you will find the entire text of the Song of Solomon with my commentary and notes of explanation. Before you begin studying the Song itself, however, you need to be aware of some of its unique qualities and characteristics.

Translating poetry always presents problems since rhyme and meter do not transfer well from one language to another. The matter is simplified somewhat in this Hebrew collection, however, since repetition of sounds or rhyme (assonance) is not a consistent feature of Semitic poetry. Westerners are fond of using parallel and similar sounds; the Hebrews and other Semitic people parallel similar words or ideas:

> Do not stare at me because I'm dark,
>> because I am darkened by the sun (1:6).

It's easier, therefore, to translate Hebrew into English and maintain the symmetry of the original text.

In English translations of the Song, however, it's often difficult to determine who is speaking, since in the English language we do not have many gender markers. In Hebrew it's fairly easy to determine whether the bride or groom is speaking because gender is indicated within the language itself (i.e., in the grammatical form of words that denote gender apart from pronouns such as he and she, him and her). So, to help you unravel the "mystery of the persona," as one commentator describes it, I've headed each poem or section stanza with the terms "Solomon" or "Shulamite" or "Daughters of Jerusalem" (the young women of the city, attributed in the NIV and other translations to "Friends") to indicate who is speaking. It's my belief that these women are the society in which Shumalite moves, the younger, impressionable women whom she instructs in the art of love. The "friends" of the young man, mentioned only once (1:7), may be a similar group of young men.

Despite what one writer calls "the charming confusion of the Song," I think I can identify twenty-five separate poems, based to some extent on the divisions in the Hebrew Bible, but also on the basis of content. As I indicated, these poems do not tell a story; rather, they allude to one and view it from a number of perspectives. I consider these individual poems to be vignettes—little pictures of love. I would also note that the divisions in some cases may seem arbitrary and perhaps they are, but this is my way of viewing the collection.

I have chosen to annotate the poems with brief notes rather than write an extended commentary because I believe the poems easily yield up all the richness of meaning and experience described in them without explanation, *as long as we grasp the imagery they contain.* The symbols and metaphors found in them are foreign to us because they come from another time and place, but once explained we can understand at once what the poet is seeking to convey. More importantly, when read from beginning to end without extensive commentary, the poems create a cumulative effect and combine to yield the purpose of the Song as a whole—and the Song does have a purpose, as we shall see.[13]

Finally, I am intrigued by the idea that this collection of poems is called a "song." Music has always been a language much deeper than words for human beings. Great music suggests something profoundly mysterious and, at the same time, profoundly meaningful. Yet that meaning, while obviously true, can seldom be translated into words. (I cannot explain, for example, why Barber's *Adagio* moves me as it does.) So it is with this love song and the "sweet mystery of love."

It may be that music was the original language. C. S. Lewis (in *The Magician's Nephew* where Aslan, the great lion, sings the universe into existence), and J. R. R. Tolkien (in *The Silmarillion*) thought so, an idea that goes back beyond them, at least to Pythagoras and his "music of the spheres."[14] Therefore, it may be that the Song of Songs was sung in "the beginning" and ultimately goes back to the eternally loving heart of God. If this is so, it is, as the poet George Herbert suggested, a way "to tune our breasts to make his music better."[15] This, at least, is my prayer.

Now on to the incomparable Song.

---

[13] Solomon's delightful lyrics, as the popular song goes, "make the medicine go down." Or, as George Herbert wrote, "Rhyme thee to good and make a bait of pleasure. / A verse may find him, who a sermon flies, And turn delight into a sacrifice." The 16th century poet Sir Philip Sidney makes the same point in his definition of poetry, which, he says, delights as it teaches. It serves "to move men to take that goodness in hand, which without delight they would fly as from a stranger" (*A Defense of Poesie* [Ponsonby, 1595]).

[14] "There is geometry in the humming of the strings. / There is music in the spacing of the spheres" Pythagoras (582?–500? BC).

[15] George Herbert, "The Temper," *The Country Parson, The Temple.*

1

Title

1:1   **Solomon's Song of Songs**

Shulamite:

1:2   Let him kiss me[1] with the kisses of his mouth—
        for your love[2] is more delightful than wine.[3]

1:3   Pleasing is the fragrance of your perfumes;
        your name[4] is like perfume poured out.

    No wonder the maidens[5] love you!

1:4   Take me away with you[6]—let us hurry!
    Let the king bring me into his chambers.[7]

Daughters of Jerusalem:

    We rejoice and delight in you;
        we will praise your love[8] more than wine.
    How right[9] they are to adore you!

1   The bride's yearnings are put into the subjunctive mood, the mood of desire, longing, and contrary-to-fact wishing: "Oh, that you would kiss me…" The stem of the verb "kiss" suggests repetition: "Kiss me again and again!" or intensity: "Kiss me passionately." A Canaanite poem reads, "He bent, their lips kissed / Lo their lips were sweet, / Sweet as grapes" (Ugaritic Texts [UT] 23 [52], 49–51).

2   The plural noun *dodhim*, which occurs six times in the collection and is translated "love," is a comprehensive term for "lovemaking," or physical sexual relationships (Cf. Proverbs 5:19: "A loving doe, a graceful deer—may her breasts satisfy you always, may you ever be captivated by her *love*." And Proverbs 7:18: "Come, let's drink deep of *love* till morning; let's enjoy ourselves with *love!*" See also Ezekiel 16:8, 23:17; Hosea 8:9 (Harris, Archer, and Waltke, *The Theological Wordbook of the Old Testament,* III [Chicago: Moody Press, 1980], 151).

3   Note that the Shulamite first speaks *of* her groom and then *to* him, a grammatical shift in persons that is common in Hebrew poetry.

4   "Name" in the Bible reflects a person's characteristic traits. Here it refers to the attractiveness of the groom.

5   The word "maiden" indicates a young woman of marriageable age. Used in the sense: "*Any woman* would love you."

6   "*Draw* me after you!" Love must be *freely* given and *freely* accepted. You cannot coerce, push, carry or pull someone into love. The lover here takes the initiative, but she responds with equal freedom. "To be drawn is as free a choice as to draw. To come is as free as to say, 'Come'" (Peter Kreeft, *Three Philosophies of Life* [San Francisco: Ignatius Press, 1989]).

7   The inner chamber of a Bedouin tent. A secret hiding place. The same idea occurs in a Sumerian marriage song: "Bridegroom, let me give you my caresses, / In the bedchamber, honey filled, / Let us enjoy your goodly beauty." Since most of the groom's/bridegroom's encounters take place out-of-doors this word may be part of the vocabulary of make-believe and designate a sheltered place in the woods or vineyard where they meet.

8   Again, *dodim* is lovemaking.

9   An adverb: "Rightly/Truly do they adore you!" i.e., "Any woman in her right mind would adore you!"

2

Shulamite:

1:5   Dark am I, yet lovely,[10]
         O daughters of Jerusalem,[11]
         dark like the tents of Kedar,[12]
         like the tent curtains[13] of Solomon.

1:6   Do not stare at me because I am dark,
         because I am darkened by the sun.

         My mother's sons[14] were angry with me
         and made me take care of the vineyards;
         my own vineyard[15] I have neglected.

1:7   Tell me, you whom I love, where you graze your flock
         and where you rest your sheep at midday.[16]
     Why should I be like a veiled woman[17]
         beside the flocks of your friends?

Daughters of Jerusalem:

1:8   If you do not know, most beautiful of women,
         follow the tracks of the sheep
         and graze your young goats
         by the tents of the shepherds.[18]

10   This line suggests ambivalence, one of the motifs in the poems. Among ancient people, dark skin was not considered attractive. Yet the Shulamite is lovely (desirable). (The Septuagint, the Greek translation of the Old Testament, translates this "black am I *and* beautiful.") A similar idea occurs in a Greek poem: "Charming Bambyce, though some may call you thin, / And blame the color of your skin, / Yet I the luster of your beauty own" (Theocritus, *Idyls* 10:26–28).

11   The "daughters of Jerusalem" are the young women of Israel and are addressed frequently throughout the poem (e.g., 2:7; 3:5, 11; 8:4, and elsewhere). They are an imaginary, rhetorical audience. In some translations they are called "friends."

12   The Kedarites were nomadic North Arabian Bedouins who dwelt in black goat hair tents.

13   The exquisite wall hangings of Solomon's court.

14   "My mother's sons" designates her *own* brothers (half-brothers would be called "my father's sons").

15   "My vineyard" or "My very own vineyard which is mine," i.e., "my *self*." A vineyard/field/garden is a well-established symbol in ancient poetry for a young woman, while "cultivating" a vineyard/field/garden is a metaphor for lovemaking. The Egyptian Amarna Letters refer to a woman without a husband as an "untilled field." Another Egyptian text describes the amorous adventures of a young military officer who is frustrated by a young woman who "guards her vineyard." A Canaanite poem from Ugarit has the groom say of his prospective bride: "I will make her field a vineyard, / the field of her love into an orchard." This is the central theme of a Sumerian marriage poem: "My sister, I would go with you to my field. / My sister, I would go with you to my garden."

16   Actually, "*this* noon," i.e., "today." Noon was siesta time when shepherds found shade and water for their sheep and for themselves and rested for several hours. And so, a meeting place for the lovers. Virgil: "And now the sun had reached his midmost toils, / When to the thick shade drove the swain his flock" (*Culex* 103).

17   "Veiled woman"—a camp follower and not the one the shepherd loves.

18   This is an answer to her question: "Where do you rest your sheep at midday?"

3

Solomon:

1:9 I liken[19] you, my darling,[20] to a mare
   harnessed to one of the chariots of Pharoah.[21]

1:10 Your cheeks are beautiful with earrings,
   your neck with strings of jewels.[22]

1:11 We will make you earrings of gold,
   studded with silver.

19   The verb suggests repetition: "I often compare you," or intensity: "I vividly compare you!"

20   "My darling" or "my friend" is a term of affection like our term "girlfriend," used to imply a special relationship. It's worthy of note that Shulamite is variously called "friend" (*ra'yah*) 1:9,15; 2:2,10,13; 4:1,7; 5:2; 6:4) "bride (*kallah*) 4:8,9,10,11,12) and "my sister" (*'achothi*) 4:12. The singular noun "beloved" (*dodh*) is the consistent term for the young man.

21   The situation envisioned actually occurred in a campaign by the Egyptian Pharaoh Tuthmoses III at Qadesh. On a tomb wall in Thebes an Egyptian soldier, Amenemheb, relates how the Prince of Qadesh released a mare among the Egyptian cavalry. Their chariots, like all nations in antiquity, were drawn by stallions hitched in pairs. The excited stallions stampeded and created chaos. *The Good News Bible* translates: "You, my love, excite me as a mare excites the stallions of Pharaoh's chariots." The actual phrase in Hebrew is: "I liken you my darling to a mare *among* the chariots of Pharaoh."

22   Costume jewelry ("bling-bling") contrasted with earrings of gold and silver.

Shulamite:

 1:12 While the king[23] was at his table,[24]
      my perfume[25] spread its fragrance.
 1:13 My lover is to me a sachet of myrrh[26]
      resting between my breasts.
      My lover is to me a cluster of henna blossoms[27]
      from the vineyards of En Gedi.[28]

Solomon:

 1:15 How beautiful[29] you are, my darling!
      Oh, how beautiful!
      Your eyes are doves.

Shulamite:

 1:16 How handsome you are, my lover![30]
      Oh, how charming!
      And our bed is verdant.

Solomon:

 1:17 The beams of our house are cedars;
      our rafters are firs.[31]

23 Note the shift from pastoral to royal terminology. This is common in poetic symbolism.

24 Literally, "his reclining."

25 "Nard"—a plant native to India. The aromatic oil extracted from it was costly and highly prized.

26 "Myrrh"—an aromatic gum. Women in ancient times wore sachets filled with aromatic spices suspended around the neck and hanging between their breasts under their dresses. Here the poet describes the union and trust that exist between the lovers, their reclining together on a fragrant couch and slowly passing the night hours. An Egyptian love poem uses a similar reference: "I have slept in the bosom of my beloved."

27 "Henna blossoms"—a shrub with delicate bluish-yellow flowers. The blossoms are profuse and fragrant. "These flowers diffuse the most gracious fragrance . . . Women take pleasure in adorning their persons . . . with these delightful blossoms" (Pliny, *Natural History* 12:24).

28 "En Gedi"—a lush oasis on the western shores of the Dead Sea, famous for its palm and balsam trees. A fresh-water spring and warm climate provide conditions for extraordinary fertility.

29 The same word is translated "handsome" in 1:16.

30 "You are beautiful *indeed*, my lover . . ."

31 He likens their bedchamber to a cool, leafy bower, over–laced with cedar and fir fronds.

5

Shulamite:

   2:1   I am a rose of Sharon,
            a lily of the valleys. [32]

Solomon:

   2:2   Like a lily among thorns
            is my darling among the maidens.

Shulamite:

   2:3   Like an apple tree among the trees of the forest
            is my lover among the young men.
        I delight to sit in his shade,
            and his fruit is sweet to my taste. [33]

   2:4   He has taken me to the banquet hall, [34]
            and his banner [35] over me is love.

   2:5   Strengthen me with raisins, [36]
            refresh me with apples, [37]
            for I am faint with love.

   2:6   His left arm is under my head,
            and his right arm embraces me.

   2:7   Daughters of Jerusalem, I charge you
            by the gazelles and by the does of the field: [38]
        Do not arouse or awaken love [39]
            until it so desires. [40]

32 The "rose of Sharon" is a crocus, a common wildflower of the Holy Land; the "lily" is a red annual that grows in profusion in the countryside. "My beauty is ordinary," she insists, "like a common wildflower." "Like a lily among thorns," her lover compares and assures her (2:2).

33 "In his shade I have often lingered, tasting the fruit" (Ariel Bloch). A delicate euphemism for lovemaking (cf., 4:12–16).

34 His "house of wine," referring to the intoxicating effects of his love.

35 "His banner"—from a root word meaning "to suspend." An awning that provides shade, or a covering.

36 Raisins were considered aphrodisiacs in the ancient world.

37 From a word that means both "to blow" (of wind) and "to exhale a pleasant odor, to be fragrant." Probably referring to the fragrance of apple blossoms.

38 Gazelles and does, because of their grace and elegance, are emblematic of a woman's beauty.

39 "Arouse" and "awaken" are the same verb in two forms, literally: "Do not cause arousal (be the agent of it) nor allow others to arouse it."

40 Literally "*the* love," i.e., "a love like this," the love she has been describing in her poems. The bride uses this "oath formula" to impart insight to the young women of Jerusalem, warning them against stirring up "this kind of love" *before the proper time.* The oath is repeated in 3:5 and 8:4. The "proper time" will be revealed in another poem.

6

Shulamite:

2:8   Listen! My lover!
        Look! Here he comes,
    leaping across the mountains,
        bounding over the hills.

2:9   My lover is like a gazelle or a young stag.[41]
        Look! There he stands behind our wall,
    gazing through the windows,
        peering through the lattice.

2:10   My lover spoke and said to me,
        "Arise, my darling,
        my beautiful one, and come with me.[42]

2:11   See! The winter is past;
        the rains are over and gone.[43]

2:12   Flowers appear on the earth;[44]
        the season of singing has come,
    the cooing of doves[45]
        is heard in our land.[46]

2:13   The fig tree forms its early fruit;
        the blossoming vines spread their fragrance.[47]
    Arise, come, my darling;
        my beautiful one, come with me."

41 The figure of a gazelle or stag (2:9,17; 8:14) suggests speed and haste and represents the maiden waiting impatiently for her lover. "Leaping" and bounding" (2:8) are intensive in form.

42 The calls of the young husband to his wife (2:10), his "coming into the garden" (4:12 ff.) to eat its "choice fruits" (4:16) or to "feed among" and "gather" the lilies (2:1–2; 4:5; 6:2; 7:3) are all lyrical representations of physical love.

43 Winter is the rainy season in Israel. Spring begins when the rainy season ends, in March or April.

44 Literally, "on the ground," i.e., when flowers cover the ground.

45 The turtledove is a migratory songbird that winters in the Sinai and makes its appearance in the spring (Jeremiah 8:7). The King James Version translation, the "voice of the turtle," has amused and puzzled many modern readers, but in the seventeenth century the word meant "turtledove." In an Egyptian love song the "voice of the swallow" calls the loved one into the fields to find her lover. But, she replies, "I have found my brother . . . and my heart is still more glad when he said to me, 'I shall not go away'" (James B. Prichard, *Ancient Near Eastern Texts* [Princeton: Princeton University Press, 1969], 468).

46 Note "*our* land." Love shuts out everyone but the one loved.

47 Harbingers of spring, The rainy season is over; the meadows are strewn with flowers, the birds are singing, the blossoms are spreading their fragrance in the air. It is the time "when a young man's fancy turns to love."

7

Solomon:

2:14   My dove[48] in the clefts of the rock,[49]
       in the hiding places on the mountainside, [50]
    show me your face,[51]
       let me hear your voice;
    for your voice is sweet,
       and your face is lovely.[52]

2:15   Catch for us the foxes,
       the little foxes
    that ruin the vineyards,[53]
       our vineyards that are in bloom.[54]

48 One of the lover's many affectionate terms for the Shulamite, his beloved (2:10,13; 4:1,10,12; 5:2; 6:9).

49 Doves in the East make their nests in the clefts of cliffs, to which they flee for protection. "As when the falcon wings his way above, / to the coven speeds the frightened dove" (Homer, *Iliad*, 21.493).

50 "In secret, steep (inaccessible) places"—a hidden, protected environment.

51 Literally, "what is seen with the eye." The noun "face" is plural, suggesting "all aspects of your beauty."

52 "Lovely"—"denotes the state of being beautiful" (*Theological Wordbook of the Old Testament*). Literally, "Your sight is beautiful," meaning, "You are lovely to look at" (cp., Song 1:5).

53 Foxes were numerous in the Holy Land and ran in packs of two hundred to three hundred animals. They were very destructive to vineyards. "I hate those brush-tailed foxes that each night spoil Micori's vineyards with their deadly bite" (Theocritus, *Idylls* 5.112). Here the word is used figuratively of anything—a harsh word, a hard look—that will mar the fragile beauty of their love.

54 The image of a vineyard in bloom is frequently used in Ancient Near Eastern literature to portray blossoming womanhood. In one Canaanite love poem Yarik, the moon god, promises Nikkal, his lover, "I will make her field into a vineyard; / The field of her love into an orchard" (Ugaritic Texts 77:22–23, see Appendix).

8

Shulamite:

2:16   My lover is mine and I am his;
        he browses among the lilies.[55]

2:17   Until the day breaks
        and the shadows flee,[56]
    turn,[57] my lover,
        and be like a gazelle
    or like a young stag
        on the rugged hills.[58]

55 "Lilies,"— i.e., the Shulamite (cf., 2:1). Syntactically, this line is parallel with the first line of the poem, "I am his and he is mine" and speaks of the delights of mutual love. "He [the one who] browses" is the lover's epithet as in 6:3. His "browsing among" is a double entendre and a symbolic reference to the delights of lovemaking.

56 Before daybreak— i.e., all night.

57 "Turn around and around," to "cavort," or "prance about playfully." Again, a sexual entendre.

58 "Rugged hills" or literally, "Mountains of Beter." Beter means "cleft," or "cleavage," "a thing cut in two," and is probably a symbolic reference to Shulamite's breasts.

9

Shulamite:

3:1 All night long[59] on my bed
 I looked[60] for the one my heart loves;
I looked for him but did not find him.

3:2 I will get up now and go about the city,[61]
 through its streets and squares;
I will search for the one my heart loves.
 So I looked for him but did not find him.

3:3 The watchmen found me
 as they made their rounds in the city.[62]
 "Have you seen the one[63] my heart loves?"

3:4 Scarcely had I passed them
 when I found the one my heart loves.
I held him and would not let him go[64]
 till I had brought him to my mother's house,[65]
 to the room of the one who conceived me.

3:5 Daughters of Jerusalem, I charge you
 by the gazelles and by the does of the field:
Do not arouse or awaken love
 until it so desires.[66]

59 "In the nights," or "night after night."

60 "I sought" is the same verb used four times in 3:1,2 from a stem word that means "to seek repeatedly." Shulamite takes the initiative. The biblical expressions for sexual relations—"he lay with her," "he came in to her," "he knew her"—make women seem passive and acted upon, but most of the lines in the Song are spoken by Shulamite. She is Solomon's equal and often the more forthright and forceful of the two. Here, in symbol and song, she seeks *him* out for love.

61 Jerusalem is always "the city" in the Old Testament (Micah 6:9; Zephaniah 3:1), but in this case it is an hypothetical locale for her "search."

62 These are *imaginary* watchmen. All aspects of this imagery—her scouring the streets of the city in search of her lover—are symbols of Shulamite's longing and desire.

63 "This *very* one!"

64 "I clung to him and did not let him go *until* I brought him . . ."

65 "Mother's house" is an idiom for purity of the marriage bed, sanctioned by her mother. "And Isaac brought her into the tent of his mother Sarah, and he *took* her. So she became his wife, and he loved her . . . (Genesis 24:67). In one Canaanite poem a young woman, Inanna, brings her spouse, Dumuzi, "to our mother's gate" for approval. See also Song of Songs 8:5.

66 This appeal is repeated verbatim from 2:7.

10

3:6   Who is this coming up[67] from the desert
       like a column of smoke, perfumed[68] with myrrh
           and incense
       made from all the spices of the merchant?

3:7   Look! It is Solomon's carriage, [69]
       escorted by sixty warriors,
       the noblest of Israel,

3:8   all of them wearing the sword,
       all experienced in battle,
   each with his sword at his side,
       prepared for the terrors of the night.[70]

3:9   King Solomon made for himself the carriage;[71]
       he made it of wood from Lebanon.

3:10   Its posts he made of silver,
       its base of gold.
   Its seat was upholstered with purple,
       its interior lovingly inlaid[72]
       by the daughters of Jerusalem.

3:11   Come out, you daughters of Zion,
       and look at King Solomon wearing the crown,
       the crown with which his mother crowned him
   on the day of his wedding,[73]
       the day his heart rejoiced.

67 "Who is this ascending"—a stylized expression suggesting magnificence, like the sun rising in the east (cf., 6:10; 8:5 and Isaiah 63:1). The answer to the question is "Solomon and his bed!" (3:7). Here the imagery changes from pastoral to martial to underscore the strength and power of Solomon's love.

68 Exuding the aroma of myrrh and incense—literally, "white stuff," since the best frankincense was white when crushed into fine powder.

69 The noun *mitta* is the common word for "bed." "Look here at Solomon's bed!"

70 "For the fear of the night." The skilled warriors represent symbolic protection from the anxieties that accompanied Shulamite's and Solomon's wedding night. They had nothing to fear! The Jewish marriage canopy originally may have represented a shelter against demonic attacks on one's marriage night. In some ancient cultures the bride and groom were guarded by men armed with swords to ward off "night dangers." Our tradition of having bridesmaids and groomsmen may be traced back to this practice.

71 *'appiryon*—an unknown word, but it probably refers to a litter or palanquin. Palanquins were mobile couches on which riders reclined. The palanquin was covered with a canopy resting on four pillars at the corners, from which hung curtains to provide privacy. It was usually carried on men's shoulders by means of poles. Here, it is a symbolic reference to the splendor and beauty of their marriage bed.

72 Actually, "fitted out for love" (cp., Proverbs 7:16–18).

73 *chatunna*— "a wedding." A similar word appears in Canaanite literature to refer to a social contract of marriage (UT 1025). The Song thus celebrates the sexual delight of a newly married couple!

11

Solomon:[74]

4:1   How beautiful you are, my darling!
           Oh, how beautiful!
           Your eyes behind your veil[75] are doves.[76]
           Your hair is like a flock of goats
               descending[77] from Mount Gilead.[78]

4:2   Your teeth are like a flock of sheep just shorn,
               coming up from the washing.[79]
           Each one has its twin;
               not one of them is alone.[80]

4:3   Your lips are like a scarlet ribbon;
               your mouth is lovely.
           Your temples[81] behind your veil
               are like the halves of a pomegranate.[82]

74 Here Solomon describes his bride in vivid metaphors—a typically Semitic device. In the *Genesis Apocryphon*, an Aramaic document found at Qumran, Abraham tells the story of his misadventures in Egypt: "The men return to the Pharaoh and describe Sarah's features: beautiful face, supple hair, lovely eyes, pleasant nose, radiant face. He continued on describing her shapely breasts, perfect hands, and everything down to her long and delicate fingers. The men compared her to and rated her far higher than virgins and birds, and all other women alike."

75 This is probably a reference to her tresses, rather than her veil. Her eyes peer "from behind" black tangled hair.

76 He compares her eyes to the luminous beauty of a dove's eyes.

77 "Skipping" or "streaming." The word occurs in the Bible only here and in 6:5.

78 The comparison is to a flock of goats "flowing" or "streaming" down a mountainside, suggesting thick wavy hair.

79 Her teeth are pure white like washed wool. Poet Robert Burns describes a lass whose "teeth were like a flock of sheep, / With fleeces new-washen clean."

80 Shulamite has no missing teeth, which would have been unusual in those times.

81 This refers to "cheeks," rather than her forehead or temples.

82 "Like a slice of pomegranate." The point of comparison is the color of a pomegranate (red) and its smoothness. Her cheeks were smooth and rosy.

4:4   Your neck is like the Tower of David,
            built with elegance;
        on it hang a thousand shields,
            all of them shields of warriors.[83]

4:5   Your two breasts are like two fawns,
            like twin fawns of a gazelle
            that browse among the lilies.[84]

4:6   Until the day breaks
            and the shadows flee,[85]
        I will go to the mountain of myrrh
            and to the hill of incense.[86]

4:7   All beautiful you are, my darling;[87]
            there is no flaw in you.

83 Probably a well-known structure at that time, built by David as part of his defense system and celebrated for its imposing appearance. This refers to Shulamite's erect carriage and stately beauty. Warriors used to hang their shields, helmets, and other equipment on city towers and walls for ornaments (Ezekiel 27:10,11). Here the shields are emblematic of the small, round pendants of precious metal that hung from necklaces that women wore.

84 Gazelles are evocative of femininity, grace, and beauty.

85 Solomon's response to Shulamite's request (see 2:17).

86 "The mountain of myrrh," "the hill of incense"—his bride.

87 "You are *wholly* beautiful" (cp., 5:16).

12

Solomon:

4:8   Come with me[88] from Lebanon, my bride,[89]
        come with me from Lebanon.
    Descend from the crest of Amana,
        from the top of Senir, the summit of Hermon,
    from the lions' dens
        and the mountain haunts of the leopards.[90]

4:9   You have stolen my heart, my sister, my bride;
        you have stolen my heart
    with one glance of your eyes,
        with one jewel of your necklace.

4:10   How delightful is your love, my sister, my bride![91]
    How much more pleasing is your love than wine,
        and the fragrance of your perfume than any spice!

4:11   Your lips drop sweetness as the honeycomb, my bride;
        milk and honey are under your tongue.
    The fragrance of your garments is like that
        of Lebanon.

4:12   You are a garden[92] locked up,[93] my sister, my bride;
        you are a spring enclosed, a sealed fountain.[94]

88 "With me" is stressed both by its position in the sentence and by repetition. The sense is "Come close to me."

89 "Bride"—from the word *kallah,* which refers to a married woman and, properly, one's own spouse (Genesis 11:31; 38:11). The basic idea of the root word is "to bring a process to an end." It refers to the completion of the betrothal contract. It's important to keep in mind that the Song of Songs focuses on a *married* couple and not on unmarried lovers.

90 From the mountains and wilderness to a more secure locale.

91 "My sister"—meaning "wife" or "dear wife."

92 "Garden,"—means the Shulamite (4:15,16; 5:1; 6:2,11). "Gardens as maidens" is a common motif in Near Eastern literature. A modern Arabic poem reads: "The garden of your beauty in its bloom is fairer and more resplendent than a garden flower." An Akkadian (Assyrian) poem describes a lover as "one who goes down into the garden."

93 Gardens were locked in the East to prevent intrusion (Isaiah 5:5). A closed garden, then, denotes a private, unspoiled place, unvisited by strangers and reserved. In one 10th century Arabian love poem a lover compares his bride to "a fresh, ungrazed meadow, unspoiled by animals or the feet of men." Another reads, "Your cheek shines like a Damascene apple; how sweet it is to pluck it in the garden and open the garden." Shulamite is a private garden, reserved for Solomon alone. She is not a public park!

94 Cisterns and springs were sealed to prevent pollution. The terms "cistern," "spring," and "fountain" are used in the Old Testament as sexual entendres: "Drink water from your own cistern, running water from your own well. Should your springs overflow in the streets, your streams of water in the public squares? Let them be yours alone, never to be shared with strangers. May your fountain be blessed, and may you rejoice in the wife of your youth" (Proverbs 5:15–18).

4:13   Your plants[95] are an orchard of pomegranates
          with choice fruits,
          with henna and nard,

4:14   nard and saffron,
          calamus and cinnamon,
          with every kind of incense tree,
          with myrrh and aloes
          and all the finest spices.

4:15   You are a garden fountain,
          a well of flowing water
          streaming down from Lebanon.[96]

4:16   Awake, north wind,
          and come, south wind![97]
      Blow on my garden,[98]
          that its fragrance may spread abroad.

Shulamite:
      Let my lover come into his garden,
          and taste its choice fruits. [99]

95 Literally, "your branches," or "your limbs," but used in a secondary sense as we do in English for arms. He is referring metaphorically to her embrace. To be in her arms is like wandering in a paradise (the exact term he uses), sampling its fruits and luxuriating in the fragrance of exotic trees.

96 A "garden fountain" is a fountain used to water a garden. Since it flows from snow-capped Lebanon the symbol suggests a copious, continuous supply.

97 "Awake, awake, awake north wind! Awake, O south wind, come breathe upon my garden, let its spices stream out" (poet Shira Kammen).

98 Some versions attribute this to the Shulamite, but Solomon is speaking here, since "my garden" is his term for the Shulamite. She refers to herself as "*his* garden"—his alone (4:16b). The scented garden is his loved one's charms, which arouse him to love. "North wind . . . south wind" suggests a gale!

99 Shulamite responds and invites her lover to browse in his garden and taste its delights: "My lover may come."

13

Solomon:

5:1   I have come into my garden, my sister, my bride;
      I have gathered my myrrh with my spice.
      I have eaten my honeycomb and my honey;
      I have drunk my wine and my milk.[100]

Daughters of Jerusalem:

      Eat, O friends, and drink;
         drink your fill, O lovers[101]

100 Literally "my myrrh *with* my spice . . . my honeycomb *with* my honey . . . my wine *with* my milk," suggesting a crescendo of delight: "not only . . . but also."

101 The response of the daughters of Jerusalem, the young women of the city: "Drink and get drunk on love." Here again is the Hebrew word, *dodim,* for love-making.

Shulamite:

5:2   I slept but my heart was awake.[102]
Listen! My lover is knocking:
"Open to me, my sister, my darling,
    my dove, my flawless one.
My head is drenched with dew,
    my hair with the dampness of the night."[103]

5:3   I have taken off my robe—[104]
    must I put it on again?
I have washed my feet —
    must I soil them again?

5:4   My lover thrust his hand through the latch-opening;[105]
    my heart began to pound[106] for him.

5:5   I arose to open for my lover,
    and my hands dripped with myrrh,
    my fingers with flowing myrrh,
    on the handles of the lock.

102 This is a dream sequence in which "knocking" and "putting his hand to the latch" are lyrical representations of love.

103 Love "left out in the cold" is a common motif in ancient love poetry: "Fear not, said he with piteous din; / Please open the door and let me in. / A poor unsheltered lad am I, / For help I know not where to fly. / Lost in the dark and with the dews, / All cold with the wet that midnight brews" (*Anacreon* III.10). An Egyptian love song has a lover excluded from his loved one's house: "She left me standing at the door of her house when she went inside... I passed by her house in a daze. I knocked, but it was not opened for me."

104 "Tunic"—the long, inner garment, usually of linen, that she removed when she retired.

105 In ancient times doors usually had a small hole through which you reached to lift the latch. This may be a symbolic reference to love play: His initiation, her initial lack of response, his hurt and withdrawal, her "search" to draw him back again—all depict the emotional ebb and flow of love.

106 "My heart grew hot," an expression used in Canaanite literature for arousal. One translator suggests, "My heart beat wildly!"

5:6   I opened for my lover,
           but my lover had left; he was gone.[107]
       My heart sank at his departure.
       I looked for him but did not find him.
       I called him[108] but he did not answer.

5:7   The watchmen found me
           as they made their rounds in the city.
       They beat me, they bruised me;
           they took away my cloak,
               those watchmen of the walls![109]

5:8   O daughters of Jerusalem, I charge you—[110]
       if you find my lover, what will you tell him?
       Tell him I am faint with love.[111]

107 "He turned away and was gone"—to strengthen the sense of her feeling of abandonment.

108 Literally, "I went out *at his word* to seek him"—his brusque word of departure.

109 A symbolic description of her bruised feelings. An Egyptian love song from the thirteenth century BC has a similar motif: "I can not let go of thy love . . . I am beaten as far as the hills with sticks, and into the fields with cudgels" (A. Erman, *The Literature of Ancient Egyptians*, 241). An old Arab poem strikes a similar note: "A quarrel arose between me and him; (It felt like) they beat me with a thousand strokes."

110 In the other "oath" sections (2:7; 3:5; 8:4) Shulamite calls upon the Daughters of Jerusalem not to awaken "a love like this." Here the formula "I charge you" (promise me) is followed by a request to tell her lover that his bride has been awakened.

111 Literally, "love sick." In one Egyptian love poem the lover insists that "sickness has invaded me," because he has not seen his loved one for seven days. The only cure is to say to him "Here she is!" (Ancient Near Eastern Texts, 467). Poet John Donne writes of his beloved Anne: "Love–slain, lo here I lie."

15

Daughters of Jerusalem:

5:9   How is your beloved better than others,[112]
        most beautiful of women?
    How is your beloved better than others,
        that you charge us so?

Shulamite:

5:10   My lover is radiant and ruddy,
        outstanding among ten thousand.[113]

5:11   His head is purest gold;[114]
        his hair is wavy
        and black as a raven.[115]

5:12   His eyes are like doves
        by the water streams,[116]
    washed in milk,[117]
        mounted like jewels.

5:13   His cheeks are like beds of spice
        yielding perfume.[118]
    His lips are like lilies[119]
        dripping with myrrh.[120]

5:14   His arms are rods of gold[121]
        set with chrysolite.
    His body is like polished ivory
        decorated with sapphires.[122]

112 "What is your lover from [any other] lover?" or "What is unique about your lover?" the Daughters of Jerusalem ask. She answers in the descriptive poem that follows.

113 He is "better looking than ten thousand [other men]."

114 "Pure gold" describes his tan face and head.

115 His thick black, wavy hair.

116 "Deep pools" describes the deep blue color of his eyes.

117 "Washed in milk," suggests languid sensuality.

118 His resplendent beard is "A bed of spice . . . no, *towers* of perfumes!" A hyperbole that betters the previous comparison.

119 Red field lilies.

120 "Flowing with myrrh"—an idiom frequently used for gracious speech (Job 29:22; Proverbs 5:3; Song 4:11).

121 Not "arms" but "hands"—his fingers are like rolls of gold studded with chrysolite, a clear stone that symbolized his fingernails.

122 "Body" is actually "abdomen," which is compared to a polished block of ivory.

5:15   His legs are pillars of marble
        set on bases of pure gold.[123]
     His appearance is like Lebanon,[124]
        choice as its cedars.

5:16   His mouth is sweetness itself;[125]
        he is altogether lovely.[126]
     This is my lover, this my friend,
        O daughters of Jerusalem.

Daughters of Jerusalem:
6:1   Where has your lover gone,
        most beautiful of women?
     Which way did your lover turn,
        that we may look for him with you?[127]

Shulamite:
6:2   My lover has gone down to his garden,
        to the beds of spices,
     to browse in the gardens
        and to gather lilies.[128]

6:3   I am my lover's and my lover is mine;
        he browses among the lilies.[129]

123 The word "legs" refers to his calves, which she compares to marble columns set in bases of gold (his feet). Note that head, hands, and feet are described as golden, possibly a reference to a deep tan.

124 "The sight of him is like Lebanon." Shulamite compares her lover's "appearance" or "bearing" to a tall, stately cedar.

125 "His palate is sweet wine," referring to his kisses or sweet words.

126 "All of him is desirable," she says. "This is my lover; and this is my friend." (In parallel to Solomon's praise song in 4:1–7 and in answer to the question in 5:9.)

127 "Who would not seek your lover!"

128 A symbolic reference to their love play (cp., 5:1, also 2:16; 4:16; 6:3).

129 "He is not yours to seek, Daughters of Jerusalem. He is mine and I am his."

16

Solomon:[130]

6:4   You are beautiful, my darling, as Tirzah,[131]
        lovely as Jerusalem,[132]
        majestic[133] as troops with banners.

6:5   Turn your eyes from me;
        they overwhelm[134] me.
    Your hair is like a flock of goats
        descending from Gilead.

6:6   Your teeth are like a flock of sheep
        coming up from the washing.
    Each has its twin,
        not one of them is alone.

6:7   Your temples behind your veil
        are like the halves of a pomegranate.[135]

6:8   Sixty queens there may be,
        and eighty concubines,
        and virgins beyond number;[136]

6:9   but my dove, my perfect one, is unique,[137]
        the only daughter of her mother,[138]
        the favorite of the one who bore her.
    The maidens saw her and called her blessed;[139]
        the queens and concubines praised her.

Daughters of Jerusalem:

6:10   Who is this that appears like the dawn,[140]
        fair[141] as the moon, bright as the sun,
        majestic as the stars in procession?[142]

130 Now Solomon extols Shulamite's loveliness.

131 Tirzah was the capitol of the kingdom of Israel from 900–871 BC. It was a city of great beauty as its name Tirzah ("Delightful") suggests.

132 Capitol city of Judah.

133 Literally, "terrifying!" "Awesome!" we would say. (Our English word "terrific" comes from the Latin *terrificus*, "to frighten," and from the French word *terrible*.) Goethe writes, "Oh, how wildly my blood courses through my veins when, by chance, my hand touches hers or our feet touch under the table! I start away as if from a fire, a mysterious power draws me back, and I become dizzy . . . and in her artlessness and innocence she has no idea how much such little intimacies torment me." The "terror" is the terror of *awe*.

134 Literally "besiege me." The intimidating, awesome effect of a lover's eyes is a commonplace of love poetry everywhere: "Fleets and armies never me appalled, / It's to a different host I fall. / A host within thy eyes, my fair, / That lurk and ply thy arrows there" (*Anacreon* XVI).

135 The lines are repeated from 4:1b–3, except a different word for sheep, "ewes," is used in 6:6. Also, line 4:4a is omitted here.

136 An example of ascending numeration common in Semitic poetry to indicate a large and indefinite number.

137 Literally, "*one* she is (one of a kind)." The same word is used in Israel's *Shema*: "Hear, O Israel, the LORD your God is one God," i.e., the *only* one.

138 "One she is to her mother," in parallel with "pure she is to the one who bore her," suggesting a special relationship to her mother.

139 Actually, "fortunate."

140 The morning star. An ancient Egyptian love poem captures the same figure of speech: "Behold her like Sothis (Sirius) rising!"

141 "Fair" is "pretty."

142 Like an army advancing under a banner.

17

Solomon:

6:11   I went down to the grove of nut trees
        to look at the new growth in the valley,[143]
    to see if the vines had budded
        or the pomegranates were in bloom.

6:12   Before I realized it,
        my desire set me among the royal chariots
        of my people![144]

143 The garden and fruit are symbols of the Shulamite. She is a "locked garden" (4:12), inaccessible to anyone but her husband-lover; he alone is invited into her garden (4:16), and he alone enters it (5:1). He describes her as a "garden spring" (4:15), and addresses her as "one who dwells in the gardens" (8:13). (Shulamite is also associated with "vines" and "pomegranates.") "I have come down to the garden," he says (cf., 6:2).

144 This verse contains an unexplained idiom that suggests sudden elevation. It probably means something like, "I am beside myself!" or, "I am transported into rapture!"

18

Daughters of Jerusalem:

    6:13   Come back, come back,[145] O Shulamite;
               come back, come back, that we may gaze on you![146]

Shulamite:

            Why would you gaze on the Shulamite[147]
               as on the dance[148] of Mahanaim?

Solomon:

    7:1   How beautiful your sandaled feet,
               O prince's daughter!
            Your graceful legs are like jewels,
               the work of a craftsman's hands.

    7:2   Your navel is a rounded goblet[149]
               that never lacks blended wine.[150]
            Your waist is a mound of wheat
               encircled by lilies.[151]

    7:3   Your breasts are like two fawns,
               twins of a gazelle.

145 *"Shubi! Shubi!"* Literally, "Turn around! Turn around!" A call to Shulamite to turn in a circle or dance.

146 "And we will watch you."

147 "Why do you watch?" is her modest reply. "What is there to see?" This elicits Solomon's praise of her in the following poem (7:1–8). This is the only place in the Song where she is named.

148 From a verb that means "to whirl." "Mahanaim" ("Two Camps") is possibly a name given to a particular dance.

149 A rounded or "moon-like bowl."

150 Blended wine was wine mixed with spices to increase its intoxicating effect. In one Assyrian love poem a king, Shusin, describes his bride, Dabbatum: "Sweet is her navel . . . sweet is her mixed drink, her date wine."

151 A symbol suggesting softness.

7:4   Your neck is like an ivory tower.[152]
        Your eyes are the pools of Heshbon
            by the gate of Bath Rabbim.[153]
        Your nose is like the tower of Lebanon
            looking toward Damascus.[154]

7:5   Your head crowns you like Mount Carmel.[155]
            Your hair[156] is like royal tapestry;[157]
            the king is held captive by its tresses.[158]

7:6   How beautiful you are and how pleasing,
            O love, with your delights![159]

7:7   Your stature is like that of the palm,
            and your breasts like clusters of fruit.

7:8   I said,[160] "I will climb the palm tree;
            I will take hold of its fruit."[161]
        May your breasts be like the clusters of the vine,
            the fragrance of your breath like apples,

7:9   and your mouth[162] like the best wine.

Shulamite:

        May the wine go straight to my lover,[163]
            flowing gently over lips and teeth.[164]

152 The image suggests a tall, proudly erect woman who carries her head high.

153 Heshbon was a city in Transjordan perhaps noted for reflecting pools near the city gate. The Hebrew word suggests a deep blue pool and large, reflective blue eyes.

154 The symbol suggests majesty, elegance, and stately dignity. "Looking" is actually "overlooking" and suggests someone looking down from an imminence, a height.

155 The mountain on the west coast of Israel noted for its densely wooded summit and lush vegetation. The name means "The Vineyard of God."

156 This is the Hebrew word for "thrum," the warp threads that hang from a loom after the woven material is removed. Here a reference to her long hair that is allowed to swing as she dances.

157 Purple tapestry, a reference to her blue-black hair.

158 "Tresses" is taken from a word that usually refers to a water course. Here used in the sense of "streaming" hair. The idea of one who is "ensnared" or captured by a lover's tresses is common in ancient and modern love poetry.

159 "How beautiful and how lovely you are, Love, more than [other] delights!" Here "Love" refers not to love itself, but to his Shulamite.

160 In the sense of "I said to myself," or "I thought." ("I said to myself, 'Let me climb that palm tree and take hold of its branches!'")

161 This is the language of love-making expressed in gentle, pure symbolism.

162 "Your kisses."

163 Here she playfully interrupts her lover by completing his sentence. "Straight" is actually "rightly." (My kisses rightly belong to my lover [to my lover *alone*].")

164 Most translations amend the text to "lips and *teeth*," but the poem actually reads, "flowing gently over lips as we fall asleep."

19

Shulamite:

7:10   I belong to my lover,
        and his desire is for me.[165]

7:11   Come, my lover, let us go to the countryside,
        let us spend the night in the villages.[166]

7:12   Let us go early to the vineyards
        to see if the vines have budded,
    if their blossoms have opened,
        and if the pomegranates are in bloom—[167]
        there I will give you my love.

7:13   The mandrakes send out their fragrance,
        and at our door is every delicacy,
    both new and old,
        that I have stored up for you, my lover.[168]

165 "He longs for me, only me." The same word, *teshugat,* is used in Genesis 3:16 to refer to the woman's longing for the man ("Your desire will be for your husband."). Here it is the man who longs passionately and solely for his bride.

166 "*Capherim,*" here translated "villages," also means henna bushes: "Let us pass the night in the henna blossoms."

167 Throughout the Song, vines and pomegranates are symbols of Shulamite's sexuality (1:6; 4:13; 7:9; 8:2). In the present verse the association is focused on her readiness for love. "Have the vines budded (in the vineyard)? Have the blossoms opened?" She answers: "There (in my vineyard) I will give you my love (*dodim*)."

168 "I have treasured up [jealously guarded] for you—for you and you *alone*."

20

Shulamite:

8:1   If only you were to me like a brother,
      who was nursed at my mother's breasts!
   Then, if I found you outside,
      I would kiss you,
      and no one would despise me.[169]

8:2   I would lead you
      and bring you to my mother's house—
      she who has taught me.[170]
   I would give you spiced wine to drink,
      the nectar of my pomegranates.[171]

8:3   His left arm is under my head
      and his right arm embraces me.

8:4   Daughters of Jerusalem, I charge you:
   Do not arouse or awaken love
      until it so desires.[172]

169 In that culture it was deemed inappropriate to show affection in public. The only accepted display was between brother and sister. If Solomon were her brother, she could kiss him freely on the street and without shame.

170 Again, her reference to her mother's house giving purity and sanction to their love-making. Furthermore, her mother instructed her in the art of love.

171 "Spiced wine . . . the nectar of my pomegranates"—poetic terms for wine and other intoxicating juices. Note once again: "I will *give* you my love."

172 This is the third and final occurrence of the "oath formula." But here in the original language another word is used to negate the phrase and to emphasize it: "*Never* to arouse . . . *never* to awaken."

21

Daughters of Jerusalem:

8:5   Who is this coming up from the desert
              leaning[173] on her lover?

Shulamite:[174]

              Under the apple tree I roused[175] you;
                  there your mother conceived you,
                  there she who was in labor gave you birth.[176]

8:6   Place me like a seal over your heart,
              like a seal on your arm;[177]
          for love is as strong as death,
              its jealousy[178] unyielding as the grave.
          It burns like blazing fire,
              like a mighty flame.[179]

8:7   Many waters cannot quench love;
              rivers cannot wash it away.
          If one were to give all the wealth of his house for love,
              it would be utterly scorned.[180]

173 Leaning on his arm.

174 The speaker here is the young woman as the Hebrew text indicates.

175 "Aroused" or "awakened" is a Hebrew euphemism for first intercourse with a virgin bride.

176 The poetic motif of birth under a tree is common in antiquity. According to ancient myth, animals usually returned to their birthplace to give birth. Since the young lover is often compared to a gazelle (2:17; 8:14), this would be especially evocative.

177 Seals denoted ownership. A symbol of intimacy and belonging.

178 Not "jealousy" as such, but "fervor." "Absolute loyalty without jealousy is the essential thing" (Miss Chimpson in Dorothy Sayers, *Unnatural Death*).

179 Literally, "the flame of Yah (the short form of Yahweh)." Death pursues us relentlessly; Sheol is insatiable; but love has greater power: It is "the flame of Yah[weh]." In a subtle way, not specified in the text, love is a cosmic force, an insight that will be developed later in this book.

180 The sense of this verse is that love is beyond material value and cannot be purchased for any price.

22

Daughters of Jerusalem:

8:8 We have a young sister,[181]
   and her breasts are not yet grown.[182]
  What shall we do for our sister
   for the day she is spoken for?[183]

8:9 If she is a wall,[184]
   we will build towers of silver on her.[185]
  If she is a door,
   we will enclose her with panels of cedar.[186]

Shulamite:

8:10 I am a wall,
   and my breasts are like towers.[187]
  Thus I have become in his eyes
   like one bringing contentment.

181 The legal term for a minor (a girl up to twelve years and a day).

182 Immature: has not reached "the age for lovemaking" (Ezekiel 16:7,8).

183 By prospective suitors.

184 Inaccessible.

185 Reward her.

186 Protect her.

187 A symbol of maturity. She is inaccessible to any but her lover. A wall like the "locked garden" gives the sense of enclosure. Only her lover has the key.

Shulamite:

8:11   Solomon had a vineyard in Baal Hamon;[188]
        he let out his vineyard to tenants.
      Each was to bring for its fruit
        a thousand shekels of silver.[189]

8:12   But my own vineyard is mine to give;[190]
        the thousand shekels are for you, O Solomon,
        and two hundred for those who tend its fruit.

188 A place name unknown to us. It suggests an especially sunny and fruitful location.

189 Isaiah 7:23 mentions a vineyard of 1,000 vines valued at a thousand pieces of silver. It seems then that a vine was normally valued at one piece of silver, hence this is a vineyard of 1,000 vines—a very valuable property. It is also possible that this was the customary bride price. See Appendix, footnote 8.

190 "My vineyard" (as in 1:6) in parallel with his. "My own"—my heart and soul to give; not to let out to other tenants but to Solomon alone.

Solomon:

8:13   You who dwell in the gardens
          with friends in attendance,
          let me hear your voice!

Shulamite:

8:14   Come away,[191] my lover,
          and be like a gazelle[192]
       or a young stag[193]
          on the spice-laden mountains.[194]

191 The verb suggests swift movement. The *New English Bible* translates, "Come into the open!" One pictures here the swift and stately approach of a young stag.

192 Emblematic of graceful movement.

193 A stag in its prime.

194 This entire verse is another example of double entendre: the play of young animals is analogous to love-play. In one Babylonian poem the lover is described as a stag, a hind, and a gazelle as he cavorts with his loved one.

THE JOY OF SEX

Sex is good. If anyone claims that it is not, the Bible contradicts him immediately.
— C. S. LEWIS, *The Letters of C. S. Lewis*

The Bible gets a good deal of bad press these days with claims that it is sexually repressive, but the charge is unfair. Scripture abounds with allusions to human sexuality. The joy of sexual union is fully embraced, clearly acceptable, and blessed. It is, in fact, celebrated as one of the wonders of the world:

> There are three things that are too amazing[1] for me,
>   four that I do not understand:
> the way of an eagle in the sky,
> the way of a snake on a rock,
> the way of a ship on the high seas,
> and the way of a man with a maiden.[2]
>   —PROVERBS 30:18—19

The Hebrew text of the last line contains a subtle grammatical nuance. Literally it reads, "the way of a man *in* a maiden." This is not a crude reference to sexual intercourse, but, as the rabbis said, a subtle allusion to the deep mystery by which a man and a woman become one flesh. "What mystery is this . . . !" the Talmud comments.[3] To this, the wisdom of Proverbs adds a practical moral point: "This is the *way* of an adulteress: She eats and wipes her mouth and says, 'I've done nothing wrong.'"[4] In other words, equally incomprehensible is the lack of sensibility in those who see nothing remarkable or

---

[1] The word in the original language means "something that causes amazement or evokes wonder."

[2] This is a "proverb of ascending numeration." It leads through three examples of mystery in order to emphasize a fourth. The word "way" is repeated in each case to underline the final example: a "way" that is beyond our understanding.

[3] *Daat Mikra.*

[4] Proverbs 30:20 (emphasis added).

mysterious about sex. To them it is a physical act like eating and drinking. Having sex is like having a meal. Nothing more.

The command in Genesis to husband and wife to be united and become "one flesh"[5] is a phrase meant to be understood both mystically and literally, and on a literal level is clearly a metaphor for marital sexual union.[6] Furthermore, according to Old Testament Law it is a husband's loving duty to fulfill his wife's "marital (conjugal) rights."[7] The apostle Paul says of these rights: "The wife's body does not belong to her alone but also to her husband. In the same way, the husband's body does not belong to him alone but also to his wife,"[8] one aspect of what Paul would call "mutual submission."[9]

The philosopher who wrote Ecclesiastes, though wary of finding ultimate satisfaction "under the sun" (in this world), sees marital love as a God-ordained consolation for the hardness and heartache of life: "Enjoy life with your wife, whom you love, all the days of this meaningless life that God has given you under the sun . . ." (Ecclesiastes 9:9). In another place, it's said of Moses that he was 120 years old, yet his eye was not dim, nor his "natural force abated," as one version translates delicately.[10] The Hebrew text reads, "his moisture was not dried up," a phrase that rabbinical scholars interpret to mean that the old man maintained his virility to the end, which in their eyes was one aspect of living to "good old age."

In images that in many ways reflect the expressions used in the Song of Songs, the book of Proverbs (5:15–19) recommends marital sexual pleasure:

> Drink water from your own cistern,
>> running water from your own well.
> Should your springs overflow in the streets,
>> your streams of water in the public squares?
> Let them be yours alone,
>> never to be shared with strangers.

---

[5] Genesis 2:24.

[6] The apostle Paul interprets the phrase on both levels. See 1 Corinthians 6:16 and Ephesians 5:31.

[7] Exodus 21:10. The noun translated "marital rights" comes from a root word that means "to answer," suggesting a loving response to a deep need for acceptance and love.

[8] 1 Corinthians 7:4–5.

[9] Ephesians 5:21.

[10] Deuteronomy 34:7 KJV.

May your fountain be blessed,
> and may you rejoice[11] in the wife of your youth.
A loving doe, a graceful deer—
> may her breasts satisfy[12] you always,
> may you ever be captivated by her love.[13]

And, of course, the Song of Songs, as we have seen, vividly portrays the joys of marital sex. Here, as nowhere else in Scripture, the romantic aspects of love find validation. This becomes even more remarkable when you realize that Israel was a society in which marriages of convenience and arranged marriages prevailed.

Unfortunately, despite this emphasis, early Christian writers ignored the plain teaching of Scripture and intimated that sexual expression was a product of the Fall. Ethicist James B. Nelson states their argument with bitter irony: "Sex is dirty; save it for the one you love."

It may surprise you to know that it was the Puritans who first rebelled against this idea. The main tenet of Puritanism was that the Bible is the final authority for life and, they noted, Scripture clearly affirms the goodness of human sexual drives and the rightness of its satisfaction in marriage.

William Tyndale, the first man to translate the New Testament into the English language, and a Puritan if there ever was one, was involved for years in a fierce debate with Thomas More, one of the English Reformers, over the issue of the celibacy of the clergy. Tyndale maintained that the Bible encouraged men and women to marry and enjoy the gift of sex.

Edmund Spenser, the English Puritan poet, refused to knuckle under to the prevailing modes of writing and chose instead to praise romantic love that culminated in marriage and sexual expression. In 1594, on the occasion of his marriage, he composed this delightful description of his "truest turtle dove."

Her goodly eyes like sapphires shining bright,
Her forehead ivory white,
Her cheeks like apples which the sun hath rudded,

---

[11] A strong word that suggests exuberant, joyful play. "Our humor toward one another is one of the most precious gifts of our humanity, and never should it play more delightfully than when we lie with each other . . ." (Henry Fairlie).

[12] A word that means to quench one's thirst.

[13] Here, as in Solomon's Song, the noun is plural and means "love-making."

Her lips like cherries charming men to bite,
Her breast like to a bowl of cream uncrudded . . .
Her snowy neck like to a marble tower,
And all her body like a palace fair,
Ascending up with many a stately stair,
To honor's seat and chastity's sweet bower.[14]

And the greatest Puritan of them all, John Milton, made his great poem *Paradise Lost*, among other things, a celebration of wedded sexual love. In depicting Adam and Eve's innocence, he disparages the longstanding tradition that the first couple did not make love in the garden and repeatedly describes their marriage in terms of sexual union. His Adam (the ideal man) uses the language of the Song to call upon Eve (the ideal woman): "Awake / My fairest. My espous'd, my latest found."[15] Later in the same poem Eve echoes the words of the beloved seeking her lover: "I rose as at thy call, but found thee not."[16]

In his work *The Doctrine and Discipline of Divorce* Milton writes: "Many waters cannot quench it [love] neither can the floods drown it." Though he attributes these words to the "spouse of Christ," he uses the passage in the Song to argue that conjugal love is a very good thing.[17]

All of these writers insisted that sex is good and prescribed the circumstance in which it is ultimately satisfying. Unfortunately, even the Puritan movement itself eventually became repressive, and the best minds of Puritanism were ignored in the Victorian Age that followed. It was during this period that people went so far as to modestly drape "the legs" of pianos and perpetrated the polite fiction that little babies were found under gooseberry bushes. And the Bible got most of the blame, even though this repression was ecclesiastical and not biblical—an important distinction.

David, Israel's poet laureate insists that delight is part of God's eternal plan: "You have made known to me the path of life; / you will fill me with joy in your presence, / with eternal pleasures at your right hand."[18] God has

---

[14] Epithalamion 25:171–180.

[15] *Paradise Lost* 5.17–25 (cf. Song 2:10,13; 7:12).

[16] 5.175 (cf. Song 5:6).

[17] 1.4 (cf. Song 8:7).

[18] Psalm 16:11. It's worth noting that our so-called "erogenous zones" have no other function than to give pleasure and arouse sexual desire.

filled the earth with pleasure, says C. S. Lewis: "things for humans to do all day long without His minding in the least—sleeping, washing, eating, drinking, *making love,* playing, praying, working."[19] All these things God has created and freely given to us for our enjoyment. But our sexual urges, however urgent, must be sanctified—put to their divine purpose—in marriage.[20] On this the Bible is incontrovertibly clear. "Abstain wholly, or wed. Thy bounteous Lord. / Allows thee choice of paths: take no byways; / But gladly welcome what he doth afford," George Herbert said.[21]

From the beginning sex and sexual relations have been linked to lifelong commitment—one man and one woman joined in marriage: "For this reason a man will leave his father and mother and be united to his wife, and they will become one flesh." In this relationship, though "both [were] naked," the man and his wife "felt no shame."[22]

Our Lord unconditionally accepted and endorsed the Old Testament teaching that sexual union is sanctioned by God in the confines of a permanently sealed marriage union: "Haven't you read," he replied, "that at the beginning the Creator 'made them male and female,' and said, 'For this reason a man will leave his father and mother and be united to his wife, and *the two will become one flesh*'"[23]—a symbolic reference to sexual intimacy. Thus Christ prescribes heterosexual marriage and the sexual pleasures that accompany it.[24] *This is precisely the point of the Song.*[25]

---

[19] C. S. Lewis, *Screwtape Letters* (San Francisco: Harper, 1996), 118 (italics added). Lewis's point in this work is that Satan creates nothing. He can only twist the good things God has created.

[20] To assert that sensual pleasures are the highest good here on earth and to make that pleasure our sole objective is hedonism, a thoroughly pagan philosophy of life.

[21] George Herbert in his poem "Perirrbanterium." A Perirrbanterium is an instrument used for sprinkling holy water (Latin *aspergillum*). Here it suggests the rite of cleansing.

[22] Genesis 2:24–25.

[23] Matthew 19:4–5 (emphasis added).

[24] Here I must point out that Jesus endorsed only *heterosexual* unions.

[25] In our secular culture things are good or evil because they have good or evil consequences. Morality, thus, is a matter of calculating costs and benefits. Others suggest that morality is formed by listening to the voice of nature within us. We gain access to this knowledge not by thinking but by feeling. Put colloquially, "If it feels good do it." The corollary, of course, is that those things that feel bad must be bad. The biblical ethic, however, is that things are good and evil because God says that they are, and only secondarily are things prohibited because they have evil consequences. That's the point of the Tree of the *Knowledge* of Good and Evil rooted in the Garden. Good and evil are defined by divine disclosure (revelation) and not through human discovery (reason and experience). Revelation takes precedence over all feelings, inclinations, and moods. Unfortunately that way of looking at morality has been lost in our day.

The Song, taken as a whole, contains a theme of *waiting* that is clearly discernible; for it is in the security of marriage alone that we experience the fulfillment of our deepest sexual longings. Thus, the poems arouse in us an eager expectation for love. Sex is something to get excited about! It is designed by God for our pleasure and for our good and is to be anticipated and celebrated, but it is an act of love that requires restraint "until the time."

Three times Solomon's bride turns from her sexual rapture and delight in her lover to give counsel to the young maidens of Israel. She chants in haiku-like simplicity: "Do not arouse or awaken love until it so desires."[26] "Love" here, as I indicated in my commentary on the poems, is not merely romance, but "love-making." Shulamite pleads with the young women of Israel to delay expressions of sexual intimacy until the appropriate occasion (marriage) for love's consummation. This refrain is a call to control passions that are aroused at the wrong time and place.

For God's children, the only appropriate occasion for sexual intimacy is marriage.[27] The complete abandonment to one another, which the lover and loved one describe in this remarkable book of poetry, is possible only when it is experienced within the total commitment and oneness that marriage alone permits.[28]

This is why sex outside of marriage is proscribed.[29] God is uncompromising in this. Illicit sex is prohibited in Scripture, not to "cramp our style" or withhold good from us, but because sex outside of marriage robs us of *authentic* pleasure. In no other sin does one feel so much of a void, for sexual

---

[26] Song, 2:7; 3:3; 8:4. Oft repeated refrains are meaningful in interpreting Old Testament literature. "Those who attend to these repetitions will find the meaning of a text revealed or clarified, or at any rate made more emphatic" (Martin Buber).

[27] In Song 5:1, where there is the most unambiguous and explicit reference to full intercourse between the married couple, they are encouraged to drink their fill and become intoxicated with love.

[28] As I have pointed out, in 1 Corinthians 6:12–20 Paul argues that a sex act creates "one flesh." To make his point he refers to a text in Genesis that has nothing to do with sex, but is about marriage. Why would he make this argument unless he understood that sex is more than a physical act? Clearly it communicates something deeper—a commitment to oneness made in marriage.

[29] Sexual sins have "more shame and less guilt," it's commonly said. "The stronger the impulse the less grievous the sin," Aquinas proposed, because, I suppose, sexual sins tend to be more impulsive, less rational and deliberate. The cold, calculating sins of the spirit (pride, self-righteousness, bitterness) are more grievous to God.

sins are not so much sins of the flesh as sins *against* the flesh—sins against the very purpose for which our bodies were made.[30] The counsel of wise men and women throughout the ages has always been that sexual virtue is always more "happifying" than sexual vice.[31] We must yield to what is right for our own present and eternal good.

And it is possible to control our natural instincts; otherwise God would not ask us to do so. Our sexual urges may have a powerful feel and force, but we are not obligated to give in to them. We can exercise self-control; we can wait.

The Daughters of Jerusalem sing: "We have a sister / Whose breasts are not grown. / What can we do to ready her for love?[32] The Shulamite responds: "If she is a wall / we'll reward her with silver; / But if she's a door / we'll protect her with cedar."[33] If she is "a wall" (that is, if she is sexually restrained) she is to be rewarded, but if she is a "door" she must be protected from harm—kept from those who would harm her.

Shulamite's example speaks for her wisdom: "I am a wall, / and my breasts are like towers. / And so I found rest [satisfaction] with the one that I love."[34] Though physically mature, Shulamite keeps herself pure before marriage. C. S. Lewis somewhere has written, "For any happiness, even in this world, quite a lot of restraint is going to be necessary . . ." Nowhere is that more true than in sexual passion.[35]

Thus, according to Shulamite, the best preparation for sexual joy in marriage is to have no sexual experience at all before marriage, an idea that seems quaint and naïve these days. As C. S. Lewis pointed out in *The Screwtape Letters,* one of the primary attacks on sex today is to picture virginity as prudery. The demon Screwtape tells his nephew, Wormwood, that one of the solid triumphs of the past hundred years is the meaning given to the word "Puritanism." "By it," he says, "we have rescued thousands of humans from temperance, chastity and sobriety of life."

---

[30] I Corinthians 6:17–18.

[31] Happiness is more than a subjective feeling; it is objective "blessedness" or spiritual well-being.

[32] Song, 8:8.

[33] Song, 8:9a.

[34] Song, 8:10–11 (my translation). Literally, "I was in Solomon's eyes as one who found peace."

[35] "'Tis chastity, my brother, chastity: She that has that is clad in complete steel" (John Milton).

Sexual experience before marriage has nothing to do with a fulfilling and satisfying intimacy in marriage. To the contrary, it empties us of our capacity for loyalty until we become incapable of forming an enduring relationship with one person. It makes us less satisfied with the partner we have and more susceptible to temptation after marriage, an idea Rudyard Kipling captures in his piercing little poem, "The Ladies":

I've taken my fun where I've found it,
    an' now I must pay for my fun,
For the more you 'ave o' the others,
    the less will you settle to one.

Furthermore, far from enhancing love, premarital sex diminishes it. Sex becomes the center of the relationship and prevents the cultivation of other aspects of friendship that enhance the relationship and make it more enduring. Sex becomes a centrifugal force that tears the relationship apart. Love turns into loathing. Nowhere is that more vividly illustrated than in the Old Testament story of Amnon and Tamar.[36]

Amnon was the son of Ahinoam, one of David's wives; Tamar was the daughter of Maacah, another of David's wives. "In the course of time," Israel's historian tells us, "Amnon son of David fell in love with Tamar, the beautiful sister of Absalom son of David."[37] Therein lies the tale.

I won't retell the story; you can read it for yourself. For our purposes here, it's enough to say that Amnon sexually assaulted Tamar.[38] Then Amnon's passion turned to revulsion: "He called his personal servant and said, 'Get this woman out of here and bolt the door after her.'"[39]

Our English versions don't, and perhaps can't, capture the deep contempt expressed in the Hebrew text. The phrase "this woman" is simply "this," a demonstrative pronoun that refers to a thing and not to a person. ("Get this out of here.") The dehumanizing word is followed in the Hebrew text with a contemptuous expression, *me'alai*, used to dismiss one whose presence is unusually offensive or obnoxious. There is no more poignant

---

[36] 2 Samuel 13.

[37] 2 Samuel 13:1.

[38] Literally, "slept": the word the Greek Old Testament, the Septuagint, chose to use to translate a Hebrew word that means "to have conjugal rights."

[39] 2 Samuel 13:17.

statement in the whole of the Old Testament than the author's commentary: "The hatred with which he hated her was greater than the love with which he loved her."[40] One rabbi notes that Amnon simply "projected on to Tamar the hatred which now he felt for himself."

Shakespeare makes the same point in one of his sonnets:

Th' expense of spirit in a waste of shame
Is lust in action, and till action, lust
Is perjur'd, murd'rous, bloody, full of blame,
Savage, extreme, rude, cruel, not to trust,
Enjoy'd no sooner but despised straight,
Past reason hunted, and no sooner had,
Past reason hated as a swallowed bait
On purpose laid to make the taker mad. . . .[41]

Shakespeare breaks lust down into its "before" and "after" components and concludes that lust leads to actions that deplete us of "spirit" (a sense of self-respect and well-being) and then to shame and self-loathing. We despise ourselves *and* the objects of our passion.

So, with great insight and wisdom, Shulamite argues for restraint—waiting, banking the flames—for sex demands the exclusivity, the privacy, and the protected environment of a loving, lifelong commitment in marriage. Simply put, sexual expression is a titanic force that demands containment. As the Song puts it, "Love is as strong as death, / as inexorable [in its demands] as the grave. / It burns like a blazing fire, / like the consuming flame of Yahweh!"[42] Its power and passion can only be harnessed within the confines and commitment of marriage. Let me explain.

MARRIAGE BEFORE SEX

According to Genesis, God created marriage, and then sex to serve the purposes of marriage. Secular social scientists would put it the other way around: sex came first, and marriage developed later as a human invention to manage

[40] 2 Samuel 13:15.
[41] William Shakespeare, Sonnet 129, 1–8.
[42] Song, 8:6b (my translation).

human sexuality. But from a biblical standpoint that's not true. Marriage came first and sexual intimacy came later, given as a "language of love" within that relationship—a natural, instinctual language built into the human psyche.

What makes sex meaningful is the meaning of sex. With sexual intercourse we "say" something with our bodies: "I am entering into your life, giving myself completely to you, holding nothing back. My whole existence belongs to you and to no one else." Sex is the "language" that communicates absolute commitment; it finds its place in marriage and nowhere else.

Sexual intimacy, thus, is the means by which we communicate the very nature of marriage itself. It is a unique experience in which we give ourselves totally, in covenant, to one person. "I will love you as long as I shall live. No one else can have my love. You *alone* have this special place in my life." This is the "promise" we make when we make love.

David Atkinson writes, "To say physically, 'I am giving myself to you,' while emotionally and spiritually holding back from covenanted commitment is in fact to live a lie—a split in the personality which is ultimately stressful and destructive."[43]

Stressful? Destructive? Who of us can deny it![44] Those who pretend that sex is only a physical act deceive only themselves.

Two people meet in a bar or at a party and decide to go to a motel or an apartment and have "meaningless" sex—no strings attached—but afterward they feel an inexplicable emptiness. Why? Because they have "lied" to each other. By their intimate act they have said, "You are special, unique, my *only* one. I give myself to you fully"; yet they have made no authentic commitment, no real giving of themselves. They do not belong to each other. They feel frustrated, cheated, and disillusioned.

George McDonald states these emotions well:

Alas! how easily things go wrong!
A sigh too deep, or a kiss too long,
And then comes a mist and a weeping rain,
And things are never the same again.

---

[43] David Atkinson, *The Message of Proverbs* (Downers Grove, Ill.: InterVarsity Press, 1997), 77.

[44] In 1 Corinthians 6:16 Paul makes the point that even the most casual sexual liaison between a man and a prostitute partakes of something spiritual.

Of course, individuals can become so dehumanized that sex loses its meaning for them. It "says" nothing to them or to their partners. But this is a conditioned response, the result of repeatedly denying one's natural instincts and awareness. These are not people to be admired and emulated, but pitied. They have lost the joy of sex.

Of all encounters, sexual intercourse is the most intense and intimate and frightening—the one in which more than in any others we are uncovered and found out. In sexual intimacy we are stripped, laid bare, exposed. Thus the Hebrew idiom is exact: "to have one's nakedness uncovered." To be uncovered means more than being disrobed. It means, in the most intimate and terrible sense, to be discovered, to be found out, to be "known" (to use the exact biblical phrase). We are torn between the yearning to expose ourselves to one another and the fear of scorn and rejection. We will always betray one another's love in some way; no one is completely reliable. That's why sex requires the containment of a lifetime commitment—a love that, having "uncovered" us, will not let us go, that will fulfill our deepest longings to be loved "as we are." In that context alone we can be "naked and unashamed," exposed and vulnerable, yet never more at ease. This is mystery, not fully understood and only hinted at in the Word, but we must take it seriously.

In the Song the groom describes his bride as a garden "closed and sealed; / a spring untrammeled, a paradise of luscious fruits and fragrant trees. / All mine!" She belongs to him *alone*. Her lover describes her as a "garden locked up . . . a spring enclosed, a sealed fountain." She is a garden whose charms arouse her lover to browse, but she is a *locked* garden, a spring *enclosed*—a private, protected, unspoiled place unvisited by strangers and reserved for her groom alone.[45]

---

[45] Catallus, the Greek poet, uses the same metaphor and makes the same point:

> As a hid flower within a closed garden grows,
> By plow uninjured and by herds unknown,
> And fed by winds, sun, rain in beauty blows
> Till youths may wish it for their own.
> And yet if it be lightly plucked and fade,
> No youths may wish for it again,
> So dear and honored is a spotless maid.
> But if she lose her virgin bloom through stain,
> On her no youths are bent, for her no damsels fain [prefer].
> (Peter Whigham, *The Poems of Catallus* [London: Penguin, 1966].)

Shulamite is not a public park; she is a private preserve. Only as her lover's *bride* does she invite the winds to blow through her garden, to arouse him to enter her garden and "taste its choice fruits." Only then does he gather myrrh and honeycomb and drink wine and milk. Only then do the Daughters of Jerusalem celebrate their love-making: "Eat, O friends, and drink; / drink your fill, O lovers."[46]

Shulamite will give no love before its time. So she muses:

My king had a vineyard
    whose vines are worth silver
He gave it to keepers
    to care for its fruit

I have a vineyard;
    its fruit is my own.
It belongs to my lover,
    to have and to keep.[47]

NEW-FASHIONED

"But," you say, "I can't wait until marriage. I'm not able to do so."

Of course not. Whoever thought you could? The pressures are too great; the temptations are too strong. Only God can enable you to do it. He says He can, and He will. "The one who calls you is faithful and *he* will do it."[48]

Begin with the assurance that God is on your side, has been on your side all along. He knows the forces of nature and nurture that have pushed you in the wrong direction. He understands your weakness through long habits of yielding and the memories of old falls that predispose you to fall again. He knows and He cares. His compassion is infinite. Despite your failures in the past and present, He has not forsaken you. When you have done your worst and have finished, when you have repented of your sin, He is ready to begin.

Furthermore, He has fully forgiven you. We are all guilty of much and capable of much more, but long ago, before you and I did anything good or

---

[46]Cf. 4:12–5:1.

[47] Song, 8:11–12 (my translation).

[48] 1 Thessalonians 5:24 (emphasis added).

bad, God paid the price for our sins—those that were, those that are, and those that shall be. His love "covers a multitude of sins"—in fact, the accumulation of a lifetime. "There is now *no* condemnation for those who are in Christ Jesus"[49]

And there is more. Despite past failure, each day is a new beginning. Remember the distraught, disheveled woman caught in bed with a man who was not her husband, dragged before Jesus by the religious leaders when He was teaching in the temple? There she lay crumpled at His feet, exposed and utterly ashamed.

Jesus' response was, "If any one of you is without sin, let him be the first to throw a stone at her." After they had all slipped away, Jesus said, "Then neither do I condemn you. Go now and leave your life of sin." [50]

Hear Jesus say, "Neither do I condemn *you*. Go and from now no longer sin." Here is forgiveness, acceptance, amazing grace, and a fresh start. This dear woman could now rise every day "new-fashioned," as poet John Donne used to say—a pure "virgin" in Christ.[51] And so it is for you and me. As Saint Benedict said, "We are in the hands of a God who can do all things."

God knows how to draw glory from our past. Despite our failures, He is at work even now conforming some small part of us to His likeness, painting His portrait, His reproduction, His work of fine art. "God, who got you started in this spiritual adventure . . . will never give up on you. Never forget that."[52] He is never in a hurry, but He always keeps His word. He will finish the job as soon as He can. You can count on it!

God does not ask for anything without giving us the ability to comply. Be assured that grace for the next act of obedience is always at hand. Don't worry about tomorrow, or tonight. Ask for God's help; rely completely on Him. Go in calm confidence, knowing that the next step, when you take it, will take care of itself. God will see to it.

Personal purity is not the work of a moment. It will take time. "You may have to fight a battle more than once to win it," Margaret Thatcher once reminded us in another context. Stay at the task until God says you are done.

---

[49] Romans 8:1 (emphasis added).
[50] John 8:1–11.
[51] See 2 Corinthians 11:2.
[52] 1 Corinthians 1:9, *The Message*.

Don't worry about occasional failure. Rise from your falls and begin again. C. S. Lewis wrote:

> We may, indeed, be sure that perfect chastity—like perfect charity—will not be attained by any merely human efforts. You must ask for God's help. Even when you have done so, it may seem to you for a long time that no help, or less help than you need, is being given. Never mind. After each failure, ask forgiveness, pick yourself up, and try again. Very often what God first helps us towards is not the virtue itself but just this power of always trying again. For however important chastity (or courage, or truthfulness, or any other virtue) may be, this process trains us in habits of the soul which are more important still. It cures our illusions about ourselves and teaches us to depend on God. We learn, on the one hand, that we cannot trust ourselves even in our best moments, and, on the other, that we need not despair even in our worst, for our failures are forgiven. The only fatal thing is to sit down content with anything less than perfection.[53]

Augustine heard "Purity" calling to him and cried out, "Let it begin *now*." May this be our prayer as well.

---

[53] C. S. Lewis, "Sexual Morality," *Mere Christianity* (San Francisco: Harper, 1980), 101–102.

THE LOGIC OF INFATUATION[1]

Falling in love was a thing that did not suggest itself to her. If she were now in what others would consider danger, it was of a more serious thing altogether; for the lower is in its nature transient, while the higher is forever.

—GEORGE MACDONALD, *The Shepherd's Castle*

These days we use the English word *erotic* to refer almost exclusively to sexual love and desire, but the Greek word *eros,* from which our word came, was used in ancient times in a much broader sense. It had sexual overtones, but was used more frequently by Plato and other Greek writers for what we would describe today as "infatuation" or "falling in love."

Infatuation is often thought of as foolish, unreasoning affection or immature love—puppy love[2]—but actually it's a concept far more complex and complete, when rightly understood. Infatuation is that wonderful feeling of "being in love." It's a noble, burning ambition to do anything for the object of one's affection, to want nothing but happiness for that individual. It wants nothing more than to be present with the loved one and to gaze at his or her form and face. Plato called infatuation "the madness of lovers, the most happy condition of all others."

The specific word "infatuation" does not appear in the Bible, though the Song of Songs clearly alludes to infatuation and other romantic aspects of love. But infatuation is part of the order God established in creation and one of the ways He "tricks" us into marriage, as C. S. Lewis once observed. Let me explain.

Marriage involves a staggering commitment. Who would consider a lifetime of self-effacing service to one person through better or worse,

---

[1] I am indebted to my friend Dr. Jack Crabtree and a conversation I had with him many years ago for the basic components of this chapter.

[2] Our word "infatuation" comes from the Latin verb *infatuo,* "to make a fool of."

sickness or health, poverty or wealth apart from *eros*? It would be unbearable. But *eros* couples commitment with euphoria and delight and thus we are taken in, "tricked," into a lifelong commitment in marriage.

Eros, however, by its nature, is designed to wax and wane. In time, and by God's grace, it is paired with a deeper love that has a firm foundation of duty, obligation, and commitment. This is the self-denying love that makes for an enduring marriage.

Here's where our culture has gone wrong. It is obsessed with infatuation. It sings about *eros,* writes about it, makes movies and TV sitcoms about it. The stories always end with the couple in each other's arms and rapturously "in love." "This is the real thing!" they say. "We will feel this way forever!" A touch, a look, a glance across a crowded room, a moonlit night, a sudden romantic mood—this is sufficient to make infatuation last forever—a lifetime of love.[3]

Not so. Enduring infatuation does not exist; it is a myth. It is not part of the real world God created. *Eros* is a *feeling*, and like all feelings it will wane. *Eros* alone does not justify sexual intimacy. Eros is strong—"as strong as death," the Song assures us—so strong that it feels like it justifies the most intimate acts. If you are "in love," you feel as though you have a mandate to "make love." But marriage, not infatuation, justifies that conclusion.[4]

The myth of enduring infatuation is why so many marriages fail. The demands of marriage will wear away infatuation, and in the end, if that is all the relationship was based on, there will be nothing left to hold the relationship together. "The feeling's gone and I just can't get it back," they say. When the feeling is gone, many conclude that the marriage is over and begin looking for someone else who will evoke the same emotion. That's why some individuals go through one marriage after another, always looking for that elusive partner that will keep love (infatuation) alive, wishing

---

[3] Hollywood offers us constant examples of this in the way it talks about love and marriage. For example, in 2005 *People* magazine carried this headline about actors Brad Pitt and Jennifer Aniston: "Take a look back at one of Hollywood's most romantic relationships . . . while it lasted . . . an end to their storybook romance." (They were "together" for 7 years, and married 4 of those.)

[4] Furthermore, it is wrong to gratify our appetite for *eros* simply because the emotion exists. In the Christian culture a preoccupation with *eros* can take the place of lust and become just as wrong. To indulge every feeling simply because it exists is sensuality. When this happens, we can become sensual Christians, pursuing serial romantic relationships or indulging in romantic fantasies.

with Edna St. Vincent Millay that, "love were longer lived and oaths were not so brittle as they are."

A marriage cannot be based on *eros* alone. If it is, it will surely flounder and fail. Though we are drawn into love and marriage by infatuation, and though there are periods of great romance and high passion in every good marriage, lifelong commitment must be the dominant theme. And that means hard work. Love is not passive, although young lovers may *fall* in love passively. But if they are to *live* in love, they must work at it, cultivate it, and make it grow. Otherwise it will die.

One of the most moving and enviable love stories written about is found in Sheldon Van Auken's *A Severe Mercy*. In it he relives an almost mythic romantic relationship with his wife, Davy—"a love to last forever." The question Sheldon was most often asked by his readers was how he and his wife achieved such a beautiful relationship. What was their secret? His answer was surprisingly simple: hard work. "We kept our love only because we worked at it."

"Love is the *work* of love," Danish philosopher Søren Kierkegaard said. Love is work, a matter of will, not emotion.[5] To love is to wish good for another, and to will it. The choices we make naturally for ourselves we must learn to make for others, for their happiness, comfort, protection, and security.

"It is by the will that we live righteously," Augustine said, and it is by the will that we love. Love *chooses* to serve, or to suffer for as long as it takes. It seeks the highest good for its object, no matter how it feels. "Thoughts, imaginations, feelings—pay no heed to them . . . . We leave these faculties at peace."[6]

Love accepts in the object of that love what otherwise it would change: "Love is not love / Which alters when it alteration finds."[7] Love may not be satisfied with what is, but it rests in God's ability to change others in due time, as we wait. If nothing more, love will grow in us that elusive, hard-to-acquire virtue—patient endurance. Our love may not change another person, but it will certainly change us.

---

[5] This is why Jesus could command love. "No one but a fool would try to command an emotion" (Peter Kreeft).

[6] Augustine, *Confessions* (Oxford: Oxford World Classics, 1991).

[7] William Shakespeare, Sonnet 116.

Love has meaning only in so far as it incorporates the idea of continuance. In the end, the ancient words are deep wisdom: "To have and to hold, from this day forward, for better, for worse, for richer, for poorer, in sickness or in health, to love and to cherish till death do us part."

SINGLE-MINDED

Better a feeble love to God,
Than for a woman's love to pine;
Better to have the making God
Than the woman made divine.

—GEORGE MACDONALD

Given my emphasis on the exclusiveness of sexual expression within marriage in this study, I feel I must address those who are now unmarried and who may be frustrated by my understanding of the Song. It is important to see the single state in biblical perspective.

Singleness was an issue in the New Testament world and was one of the concerns Paul, being single (or divorced or widowed—we don't know) himself, had thought through at some length. His most compelling treatment of this theme is found in 1 Corinthians 7:1–24, and I suggest that you read that text before continuing.

Paul begins with this premise: "Concerning the things about which you wrote, *it is good* for a man not to marry."[1]

Some commentators would say that Paul is quoting a letter from the Corinthians and that the phrase "It is good for a man not to marry" is a quote from their letter, and that Paul then corrects their mistaken idea. But the problem with that interpretation is twofold: First, there's no evidence that the statement is a Corinthian quote—there are no quotation marks in the Greek text—so these may be Paul's very words. Second, even if Paul is quoting the Corinthians, he doesn't disagree with them. Quite the contrary. He explains that marriage is good and is one way to counteract the sexual temptation. But then, having written about a number of issues relating to

---

[1] 1 Corinthians 7:1 (emphasis added). Paul's exact word is "touch," ("not to touch"), which here he uses by metonymy for marriage. The context indicates this meaning.

marriage and divorce, he maintains that being single is also good, and is, in fact, a preferred state, at least for him. (Paul would not advocate being single and sexually active. But being single and celibate is good, he says.)

We're so accustomed to hearing that being married is good and wonderful and the ideal state that single men and women may come to believe that being unmarried is not. Some might even make the leap that since it's not good, it's sinful—or if not sinful, then at least strange. "So why aren't you married yet?" is the opening gambit of would-be matchmakers, as though something must be wrong with you if you aren't. Especially strange are those hardy souls who remain single after they're "over the hill."

And unfortunately the idea that being single is bad shows up in the church, where it shouldn't show up at all. Isn't it odd that we celebrate marriage and denigrate the single state, when our Lord—the sinless perfect man—wasn't married at all? That's very odd indeed.

Most would never openly criticize a single person, but the subtle inferences are there—the oft-stated opinion that marriage is God's will for the race, which singles can only interpret to mean that they're somehow out of God's will. Or the teaching that marriage is the norm, from which singles can only assume that they are abnormal. Or put another way: "A man can't be whole without a woman, and a woman can't achieve full status unless she's a wife and mother." All of which is nonsense. Our Lord made no such distinction; all are free to seek the abundant life. Would Jesus and His apostles teach us that singleness is a gift from God if it were a serious impediment to one's growth in grace?[2] Of course not. Yet we perpetuate the myth that single people are somehow less capable of vigorous and sturdy Christian living.

Singleness is good. For some, in fact, remaining single is the best option, as Paul makes clear in 1 Corinthians 7. The controlling theme of the chapter is stated in verse 17: "Only as the Lord has assigned to each one, as God has called each, in this manner let him walk." In other words, maintain the status quo: "Each man must *remain* in that condition in which he was called."[3]

Paul emphasizes this idea of continuity or "remaining" throughout the chapter: Those formerly married and now unmarried should remain unmar-

---

[2] Matthew 19:10–12; 1 Corinthians 7:1–8.
[3] 1 Corinthians 7:17, 20 NASB (emphasis added; cf. 7:8, 20, 24, 40).

ried (8–9); those married, should remain married; those divorced should remain unmarried, or be reconciled (10–11); those married to an unbeliever should remain married (12–16). Then, in verse 17, he gives the call to "remain"—to stay in the place in which God called you. One's state or station in life has nothing whatever to do with his or her ability to live out the life of God.

The verb "called" here does not refer to one's vocation or call to ministry or service, but rather to the call to salvation. The point Paul is making is simply that we should serve Christ in the situation in which He found us. His "assignment" (the situation in which He called us) has been made. Now our task is to live out our call to salvation in that place. Paul does not proscribe marriage after our call to salvation, but he does seem to be saying that in view of the exigencies and dangers (persecution) of his day, it is good to remain single.

Paul argues that all social states are irrelevant: one may be called as Jew or Gentile, slave or free. Ethnic differences, social differences, differences of station and position in life have no relationship to our capacity to love God and obey Him. If we are given an opportunity to get out of a difficult situation or into a different situation—if it's possible and proper to do so—we should, but we shouldn't believe that a change in status will make us better Christians, better able to reproduce the life of God in the world. There's nothing spiritually significant about the place in which we find ourselves. Being free doesn't ensure that we can have a larger sphere of influence than we can have as a slave, though it is not wrong to seek freedom. His point is this: There is no state of being that inherently hampers our capacity to grow spiritually and to influence others for the sake of the Kingdom of God.

You can see where Paul is going with this argument: You can serve God where you are. Thus, our married or unmarried state is our "assignment" (Paul's word) and the place in which we're called to grow. We're not in a holding pattern, waiting for another, better place to serve. Our present state, no matter what it is, is a place to make visible the invisible Christ.

Paul, being single, would understand the "grass is greener on the other side of the fence" mentality—the idea that we can't grow and flourish in our present state or until we resolve our single state. Such thoughts were conveyed clearly by songwriter John Fischer when he was single and described his own feelings as a single man: "The suggestion creeps into my mind that I'm incomplete; I'm flying around trying to find the airport so I can get my feet on the ground and start living. . . . It comes up even in the way I live, the way I place things in my room. I keep thinking, 'When I have my own place . . .' or 'When I have someone with me, then I'll do this or that . . .' This kind of thinking keeps me from being the man God has called me to be right now."[4]

Some think of singleness as an olive jam in a jar of olives—the one impediment that frustrates the use of their God-given abilities. They think, "When I get my singleness out of the way, all the rest of me will come out!" But that's not so. God's grace is sufficient for you now.

"Remain with God," Paul insists. That's the secret of rest when everything else is unresolved. We put our roots down into God and find rest for our souls.

Margaret Clarkson, a prolific songwriter, was single throughout her life and made the profound discovery that she was never alone because of God's presence. "To know God, to know beyond the shadow of a doubt that He is sovereign and that my life is in His care: this is the unshakable foundation on which I stay my soul. Such knowledge has deep significance for the single Christian."[5]

As Paul would say, "I have learned to be content in whatever circumstances I am. I know how to get along with humble means, and I also know how to live in prosperity; in any and every circumstance I have learned the secret . . ." And what is the secret of this endurance? "I can do *all* things through Him [Christ] who strengthens me."[6]

I'm not sure that I know what the so-called "gift of celibacy" is. It certainly doesn't mean that you won't long for a partner. And it doesn't mean that you won't ever be lonely. I would say, however, that if you are now single, *you have the gift of celibacy*. In other words, God has graciously given you the ability to live as a single person. And it is possible to control your sexual urges and other passions. You can draw deeply on the love and power of God to deal with the pressures of sexual temptation.

---

[4] John Fischer, unpublished manuscript.
[5] Edith M. Clarkson, *Destined for Glory* (New York: Phoenix Press, 1983).
[6] Philippians 4:11b–13 NASB (emphasis added).

Remember, your Lord knew the temptations and rigors of a single life. He had no life partner and no place He could call home here in earth. "Foxes have holes," He sighed, "and birds of the air have nests, but the Son of Man has no place to lay his head."[7] He understands.

Finally, far from curtailing your usefulness, your single state enables you to make the most of your time here on earth—"that you may live . . . in undivided devotion to the Lord."[8]

There are two ways to look at the brevity of life: one is to go for all the gusto here and now. Another is to see life's transience and make the most of it. Time is a rare commodity and should be spent well. The best investment of your time is to serve the interests of the kingdom of God.

Paul argues that being single gives one an opportunity to pursue God with every element of one's life. It makes possible a degree of devotion and service to Christ that a married person cannot have. An unmarried man or woman can devote his or her life wholly to knowing God and serving Him.

I think of Henrietta Meers, John Stott, and others whose energies have been totally devoted to ministry to others—to study, teaching, and writing, to discipleship and leadership. That's difficult, if not impossible, for a married person to do. Marriage brings legitimate demands and responsibilities that make it necessary for married men and women to divide their time between family and ministry—and that's as it should be. But the single person can be more flexible, can adapt more quickly, can give themselves more fully to ministry because they have less responsibility to others and for others.

The world and its obsession with sexuality has led us to develop a wholly false view of our sexuality. Our sex life is not the measure of our humanity. One can be single and celibate and still be human in the fullest sense of the word.

Elaine Morgan some years ago wrote a remarkable article on chastity in the *New York Times*. Perhaps the most startling thing about it was the title: "In Defense of Virgins." She writes about what she calls the "submerged minority" of those who are not obsessed with their sexuality. "What few people are gullible enough to believe in is virgins. Well, I believe in them. They are still around, among both sexes, and they are not all under the age of fourteen."

---

[7] Matthew 8:20.

[8] 1 Corinthians 7:35

She reminds us how people in the past sublimated their sexual energies into works of considerable achievement for the benefit of others as well as themselves. "Today we would not say that these energies had been sublimated; we would say that they have been inhibited. We have this arbitrary conviction that, if you have the biological capacity to do something and yet don't want to do it, then you are 'inhibiting' your deepest instincts, and this must be bad."

"Folderol," she says. "There is no evidence that sex is a categorical imperative like food and oxygen; and there is no evidence that voluntary abstention from it leads to neurosis or emotional disturbance."[9]

Paul's point exactly. There is a life beyond love, sex, and marriage. It is found in devotion to Christ and in His love for us. The divine image of the bride and bridegroom in the Song is for all of us.

What an immense consolation!

---

[9] Elaine Morgan, "In Defense of Virgins," *New York Times*, November 25, 1977.

KILLING ME SOFTLY

Romantic love is an infinite passion because it is an unconscious longing for the infinite God who is love.

—PETER KREEFT

George MacDonald, in *The Flight of the Shadow,* tells the story of a little girl, Barbara Whichote, who lived with her uncle and who one day went into his study when he was gone and rummaged through his private and forbidden collection of jewelry. The secret burned inside her for days, until in desperation she ran to her uncle one night. "Please uncle," she sobbed, "will you kill me?"

"Yes, yes," her uncle replied. "I will kill you my darling! . . . Like this! Like this!" Then stretching out his arms he drew her in and covered her face with kisses. MacDonald concludes with this assurance: "We have been killed by the kisses of God."

In the Song, Shulamite cries out, "Oh, that he would kiss me." Is this not the thing for which our souls hunger as well—to be gathered in, to be smothered by the loving "kisses" of God.[1]

Saint Bernard of Clairvaux writes, "O happy kiss, and wonder of amazing self-humbling which is not a mere meeting of lips, but the union of God with man." Bernard urges us to call out to God with the words of the bride: "Take me away with you—let us hurry!"[2]

---

[1] All souls are feminine. Not female but *feminine.* (The word for "soul" is feminine in Hebrew.) In the Song of Songs it is the groom and not the bride who symbolizes God, the bride and not the groom who symbolizes the soul. The reason for this is not that males are in any way superior and more "godlike," but that God, by His nature, is the husband of my soul, and I, by nature, am His bride. This is symbolic language, of course: God has no body and thus no biological sex, but the image of "husband" means something to us—is something we can grasp, and that something is the role God plays in our relationship with Him. Paul uses the same figure of speech in his letter to the Corinthians: "I feel a divine jealousy for you, for I betrothed you to Christ to present you as a pure bride to her one husband." C. S. Lewis looks at the symbol in another way. "God is so masculine," he says, "that we are all feminine in relationship to Him."

[2] *Bernard of Clairvoux,* trans. G. R. Evans (New York: Paulist Press), 216.

The Groom replies: "Arise, my darling, my beautiful one, and come with me. / See! The winter is past; the rains are over and gone. / Flowers appear on the earth; the season of singing has come, the cooing of doves is heard in our land. / The fig tree forms its early fruit; the blossoming vines spread their fragrance. / Arise, come, my darling; my beautiful one, come with me."[3]

Here we are introduced to another way of looking at the Song, a "more-than-literal" understanding in which we find God and ourselves in the poems. At this deeper level of interpretation, the poet is writing to give *us* a song and a voice, inarticulate lovers that we are. We are asked to seek not merely what the *poet* felt, but what *we* feel—to make the Song our own.

Though human lovers can sing the Song to each other, here we find it employed as a means of worship to God. This is a way the Song can be read and has been read for centuries. Thus, on one level it is a description of the purest human love we can imagine, but on a deeper level it reflects our love for God and His unfathomable love for us.

C. I. Scofield writes, "Nowhere in Scripture does the unspiritual mind tread upon ground so mysterious and incomprehensible as in this book, while the saintliest men and women of the ages have found it a source of pure and exquisite delight. That the love of the divine Bridegroom should follow all the analogies of the marriage relation seems evil only to minds so ascetic that marital desire itself seems to them unholy."[4]

Here is the synthesis, I believe, between modern writers who interpret the Song literally and traditionalists who interpret the Song as merely symbolic. We can cut across these either/or positions and rightly interpret it both/and, because all human love is a symbol and sign of a deeper human hunger for eternal love. We may deny that it exists, but in our quieter moments we *know* it is true.

Everything is about love, or the lack of it, or so we say; but *human* love is not the ultimate end that we seek. It is but the means to that end, the stimulus that triggers in us a deep thirst for God's absolute and consuming love. We are never satisfied with the affection we're given here on earth, no mat-

---

[3] Song, 2:10–13.

[4] "Introduction to the Song of Songs," *Scofield Bible* (London: Oxford University Press, 1917), 705.

ter how intense and enduring it may be. We seek something more than one another.

"Love is a journey to another land," said Anglo-Irish writer Rebecca West. She was wiser than she knew, for, put another way, romantic love and natural affections are meant to set us on a journey to find infinite love. As though we're following a river upstream, we pursue love's meandering course to its headwaters. There, at its source (God's effervescent love), we find the spring from which all human loves flow. There we find "a spring of water welling up to eternal life" from which we can slack our thirst forever.[5] This "is the end of the heart's quest and the beginning of its fullness," Aquinas said.

This, I believe, is why human love and sexual passion permeate and dominate our lives. It is God's gift to us to draw us to His everlasting love. Our passion is more than physical impulse or instinct; it is a God-designed reflection, however pale, of our passion to know Him and to be known by Him. It is no coincidence that sexual intercourse in the Bible is described as "knowing," for human sexual passion is a small representation of the chief end of man: to "know God and enjoy Him forever."

Long ago Charles Williams noted that "sensuality and sanctity are so closely intertwined they can hardly be separated." Paul said as much: "For this reason a man will leave his father and mother and be united to his wife, and the two will become one flesh [another term for sexual intimacy]." Then he concludes with this thought: "This [sexual union] is a profound mystery, but *I am [also] talking about Christ and the Church.*"[6]

Here Paul clearly links marital sexual intimacy with spiritual intimacy with God. One is a representation and reflection of the other. Thus, I say, *sex is holy*, an eloquent expression of our profound, inexpressible hunger for God, a passionate urge to merge with the object of our love and ultimately with the God who loves us as no human lover can.

That longing—to know God and experience His love—originates with God. It is His calling, His wooing that awakens us to desire. Indeed, we would not seek Him if He did not first seek us. Our longing for intimacy and union is the answering cry of our hearts to His call. "Even when men knock

---

[5] John 4:14.
[6] Ephesians 5:31–32 (emphasis added).

on the door of a brothel," said G. K. Chesterton, "they are looking for God." That hunger may be masked and distorted and misunderstood, but it is undeniably there.

Thus marital love and sex is good, but not as good as it gets, which is why God has placed limits on the depth of all human relationships. Our need for intimacy always outstrips the capacity of another human being to satisfy it. We will always betray another's love in one way or another. This is what Original Sin means: no one is completely trustworthy; no one will always "keep covenant."[7] We will always let one another down.

"An image can easily become an idol and romantic love is a powerful image," says Peter Kreeft. "We expect joy from this human experience, but it ends in bitter disappointment. We have heaped on the shoulders of our beloved a burden of joy-making only God can carry and we are scandalized when those shoulders break."[8]

That hunger—for something beyond human love—is the way God leads us to His love. In each of us there is a deep and holy place reserved for Him alone, a place that no one else, not even the greatest human lover, can ever fill. We draw near to God to find final affection. "We learn at last to love thee true and best, / And rush with all our loves back to thy infinite rest."[9]

May I suggest a journey, then, an exploration? Read each poem in the Song at a leisurely pace and put yourself in it. Meditate on each line. Make Shulamite's words your words and offer them up to God. Then read Solomon's (the lover's) words as God's words to you, and listen to His response. Hear Him speak to your heart, "Come away with me my beautiful one, my bride . . . ." The longer we stay with the symbol and reflect upon it, the more it will yield. "A symbol should go on deepening," said Flannery O'Connor.[10]

Imagine! God wants *you*, not for your body, your clothes, your talent, your intellect, your personality, but simply because you are you! He loves *you*. He cannot take His eyes from *you*. You are radiantly beautiful. "How beautiful

---

[7] The essence of sin is disloyalty to God's covenant of love.

[8] Peter Kreeft, *Three Philosophies of Life* (San Francisco: Ignatius Press, 1989), 106.

[9] *George McDonald* (New York: Collier Books).

[10] *The Habit of Being: Letters of Flannery O'Connor*, ed. Sally Fitzgerald (New York: Vintage Books, 1988), 70.

you are . . . how beautiful," He sings. "The winter of loneliness and misery is past; the time of singing has come."[11]

"Ah," you say. "How could He love poor me? I am dark with sin and guilt, loathsome, grotesque." No, you are His perfect one."[12] He sees awesome beauty in you.

"Love is blind," you say. No, *infatuation* is blind, but not God's love. He sees you as you are; yet He sings to you.

> My dove in the clefts of the rock,
>> in the hiding places on the mountainside,
> show me your face,
>> let me hear your voice;
> for your voice is sweet,
>> and your face is lovely.[13]

Is this illusion? No, it is clear-sighted love. God's eyes are filled with your beauty. He loved you before your father, spouse, or children loved you (or wounded you). "If you were the only person on earth, He would have gone to all the trouble He went to just to win *you*," one early Christian writer said. Does this not excite us?

Whatever your heart may be saying at this moment, you must know that God is the lover of your soul.[14] Even now, in your unperfected state, He cries out to you, "How beautiful you are. . . how beautiful." He yearns for you; "He hath longing to have you."[15]

---

[11] Is this not reminiscent of Hosea's love for Gomer, his bride? Is this not God calling to your soul and mine? "Therefore I am now going to allure her; I will lead her into the desert and speak tenderly to her. There I will give her back her vineyards, and will make the Valley of Achor a door of hope. There she will sing as in the days of her youth, as in the day she came up out of Egypt." God says: "I will betroth you to me *forever*; I will betroth you in righteousness and justice, in love and compassion. I will betroth you in faithfulness, and you will acknowledge [Heb: "intimately know"] the LORD" (Hosea 2:14–15, 19–20, emphasis added). Intimacy with God flows from His faithful love. Reflecting on that love draws us into His heart.

[12] Song, 6:9.

[13] Song, 2:14.

[14] C. I. Scofield comments, "It is most comforting to see that all these tender thoughts of Christ are for His bride in her *unperfected* state" (On Song of Songs, Chapter I, *Scofield Reference Bible*).

[15] St. Teresa of Avila, *Interior Castle* (various editions).

We are special objects of God's favor and affection. His is a love that swallows up every love in its fullness. The Song in this way becomes more than a love song. It becomes adoration and worship.

Worship? Yes. But at the same time the Song becomes something more—a means by which we can begin to assuage the raw passions of the flesh.[16] St. Jerome said that the bride in the Song of Songs discloses the mysteries of chastity: "My beloved is mine and I am his." This is not sophistry—reasoning that is sound in appearance only—but true wisdom, for our fiery passions were created to find ultimate satisfaction in God's love alone. They are, as the Shulamite said, the "flame of Yah," an image that poet George Herbert reflects in his prayer that our passion may "kindle in our hearts such true desires as may consume our lusts and . . . cause our hearts to pant after Thee." We can redirect our passions to the One who loves us as no other can. "Instead of lusting," we can "look up."[17]

Here in the Song "we find ravishment," Peter Kreeft writes, "the deeper and more passionate ravishment of the heart, which is capable of much more passion, intimacy, and joy than the flesh only."[18] As Israel's poet sighs, "You have stolen [ravished] my heart, my sister, my bride; you have stolen [ravished] my heart with one glance of your eyes."[19]

So John Donne prays:

> Take me to You, imprison me, for I—
> Except You enthrall me—never shall be free,
> Never ever chaste, except you ravish me.

---

[16] "Assuage," I say, and not utterly satisfy, for perfect submission and satisfaction of our sexual urges await the day when we shall see our Lord and Lover face to face.

[17] Louis Hennings, "First Kisses," unpublished poems.

[18] Kreeft, *Three Philosophies*.

[19] Song, 4:9.

APPENDIX

I have included here, for comparison, an erotic love poem from Ugarit, a city located on the Mediterranean coast of northern Syria. Ugarit was the capital of an ancient kingdom that flourished during the second millennium BC, and is known for the large library and the ancient cuneiform texts that were discovered there. Written in a language and alphabet that closely resemble ancient Hebrew, the Ugaritic texts have shed light on the Hebrew language and on the literature and culture of the ancient Near East during the thirteenth and fourteenth centuries BC. Some of this poetry is frankly pornographic, but this particular poem, "Yarik and Nikkal," is more "romantic" and has many of the words and stylistic conventions found in the Song of Songs.

YARIK AND NIKKAL

⊢⊢⊶ ⧮⧻⊫ ⊢⊯⅂⅂
I will make   her field   a vineyard

⧮⧻ ⧻⧻⊫ ⊫⊯⊶⊣⅂
The field of her love   an orchard

UT 77:24

I will sing of Nikkal[1] and ib[biha];[2]
  Of Har'hab,[3] King of Summer
Of Har'hab, King of the Autumn Festival;
  When the sun sets, Yarik[4] shines;[5]
He embraces her who will bear a son to him.

Hear, O Kotherites,[6]
  Daughters of the New Moon—Swallows,
Behold, a maiden will bear a son!
  Look! Lo! Before him she is aroused to love;
Before him she surrenders herself;
  And he will bring her into his house as a wife.

Hear, O Kotherites,
  Daughters of the New Moon—Swallows.
Yarik, Elluminator of the Heavens
  will send a bride request
through Har'hab, King of Summer.

Give me Nikkal;
  Yarik will pay the bride price for her fruit;[7]
May she enter his house
  And I will give her bride price to her father;
A thousand pieces of silver and much gold;[8]

---

[1] Nikkal was a well-known goddess in the ancient world. She was also called "Great Lady," the moon goddess.

[2] The text is broken, but probably, "her fruit." (Cp., Song 4:13,16; 7:7; 8:12.)

[3] The Canaanite god of cycles and seasons, who was the father of Nikkal.

[4] Yarik is the moon god, probably the god for whom the city of Jericho was named. Jericho was an ancient city, given its name by the Canaanites before Israel entered the land.

[5] A double entendre. The word also means "to be passionate."

[6] The Kotharites serve the same purpose as the Daughters of Jerusalem in the Song of Songs: they are an imaginary audience.

[7] Cf., Song 8:11.

[8] Cf., Song 8:12.

I will send lapis lazuli
   I will make her field into a vineyard;[9]
The field of her love into an orchard.
And Har'hab, King of Summer replies
   to the favorite of the gods: Baal's sons-in-law!
Wed Pidriya, Daughter of the Dew;
   I will bring you near to her father, Baal.
Athtar [her brother?] will intercede for you
   to acquire Yibridamy, the daughter of her father.

But the Lion [Yarik] is aroused!
   Yarik, illuminator of the Heavens,
And the favored one answers:
   I will marry Nikkal!

Afterward, Nikkal arranges to marry Yarik;
   Her father sets the arm of the balance;
Her mother the trays of the scales;
   Her brothers arrange the weights;
Her sisters the stones of the scales.[10]
It is of Nikkal and her fruit[11] that I sing.
   Yarik shines on her;
And may he shine forever.

---

[9] Cf. Song 1:6, 14; 2:15; 7:12; 8:11.

[10] For weighing out the bride price.

[11] Cf. Song of Songs 2:3; 7:7−8; 8:11−12.

NOTE TO THE READER

The publisher invites you to share your response to the message of this book by writing Discovery House Publishers, P.O. Box 3566, Grand Rapids, MI 49501, U.S.A. For information about other Discovery House books, music, videos, or DVDs, contact us at the same address or call 1-800-653-8333. Find us on the Internet at http://www.dhp.org/ or send e-mail to books@dhp.org.

ABOUT THE AUTHOR

AVID ROPER and his wife, Carolyn, offer encouragement and counsel to pastoral couples through Idaho Mountain Ministries. David is the author of more than ten books, including *Psalm 23: The Song of a Passionate Heart, The Strength of a Man, In Quietness and Confidence,* and *Out of the Ordinary.* David is a graduate of Dallas Theological Seminary and, in past years, served on the pastoral staff of Peninsula Bible Church in Palo Alto, California, and as senior pastor of Cole Community Church in Boise, Idaho.